What's
Physics
all about?

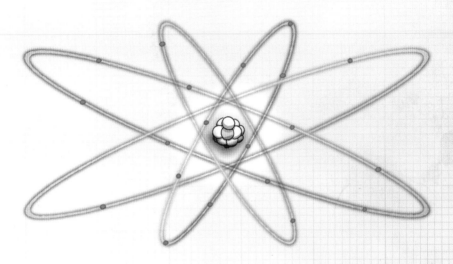

Kate Davies

Illustrated by Adam Larkum

Designed by Steve Moncrieff, Tom Lalonde
and Samantha Barrett

Physics consultants: Toby Swan and Dr. Lisa Jane Gillespie
Edited by Rosie Dickins and Jane Chisholm
Series advisor: Tony Payton

Contents

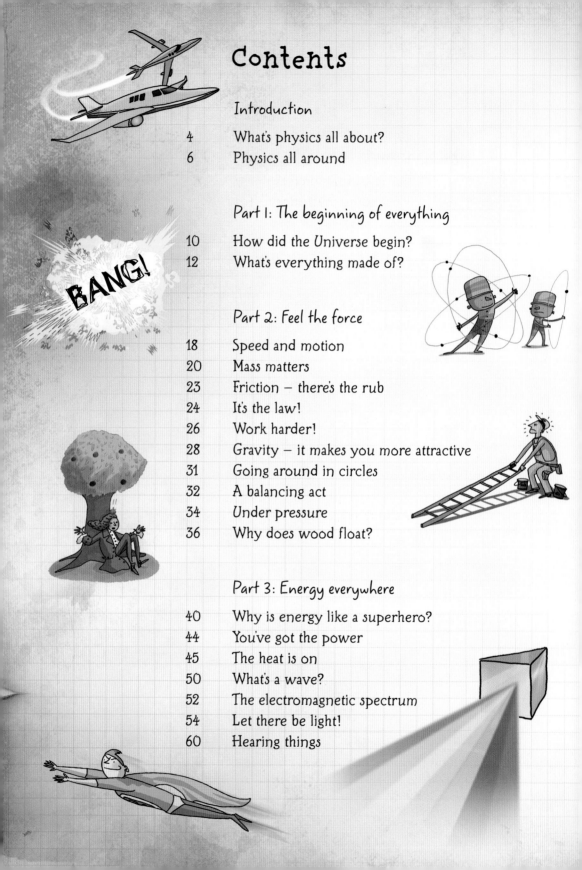

BANG!

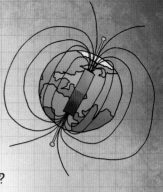

Part 4: It's electrifying!

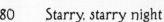

Part 5: Lost in space

Part 6: More about physics

Internet links

You can find out all sorts of things about physics on the internet. You can find experiments to do at home, design your own theme park using the laws of physics, read all about life as an astronaut, and ask a physicist a question. For links to these websites, and many more, go to www.usborne.com/quicklinks and type in the keywords "what is physics".

Please follow the internet safety guidelines displayed on the Usborne Quicklinks Website.
The links are regularly reviewed and updated, but Usborne Publishing cannot be responsible for any website other than its own.

What's physics all about?

Physics is about how things work, and why things happen the way they do. Physicists ask all sorts of questions about life, the Universe and everything, from why a teaspoon gets hot when it's in a cup of coffee, to what happens to your body when you dive to the bottom of the sea.

They also ask some really big questions...

What is the Universe made of?

Deep down, every single thing in the Universe is made from the same tiny bits of stuff called atoms.

But is an atom the smallest thing there is? And where did all this stuff come from in the first place? Physicists don't have *all* the answers, but they have lots of ideas.

How does the Universe work?

Physicists can't explain how the whole Universe works – at least, not yet. But they can explain how all the things in it work the way they do.

If you've ever wondered why there are different seasons in a year, or why things fall to the ground, the chances are physics has the answers.

Careers in physics

People who study physics don't all end up becoming scientists. Here are some of the many jobs physics prepares you for:

Architects
need to understand the laws of physics to design buildings that won't fall down.

Computer game programmers
use the laws of physics to design more realistic games.

Pilots
need to know how planes fly – which is all to do with physics.

Doctors
use physics to understand how medical technology works.

What is energy?

Energy is what makes things happen. It makes atoms move, light shine and electricity flow. If there was no energy, the Universe would be a really quiet, cold and boring place to live.

Physicists study all kinds of energy. And they try to find new energy sources so that our power supplies will never run out.

Lightning is electrical energy that flashes through the sky.

What's out in space?

Physics is about everything in our world and beyond — so physicists want to know what it's like in space.

Do things in space work in the same way that things work on Earth? Does time change if you travel through space? Physicists who try to answer questions like this are called astrophysicists. Astronomers, who study the night sky, are physicists too.

When you look at the stars, you're seeing all the way into outer space...

A journey into the unknown...

The really exciting thing about physics is that there is so much still to discover. Physicists argue about things such as whether using a mobile phone can give you cancer, and if there is life on other planets. Perhaps no one will ever know all the answers for certain, but physics can help scientists get closer to the truth.

Just a matter of time?

One day, an over-enthusiastic physicist in a lab somewhere might create a completely new universe in a beaker.

Physics all around

People have been studying physics – without calling it that – for thousands of years, and using their discoveries to make life easier along the way. The first people who invented the wheel, or built canoes, were using the rules of physics. Without physics there would be no...

...parachutes

In 1617, Croatian inventor Faust Vrancic made an early kind of parachute by strapping a curved canopy to his back. It slowed his fall when he jumped off a tall tower in Venice.

...telephones

The telephone was invented by Scotsman Alexander Graham Bell in 1876. Bell spent years investigating the way sounds are created and how they move.

...light bulbs

In 1878, Englishman Sir Joseph Swan and Thomas Edison from the USA invented the light bulb almost simultaneously. Instead of fighting, the pair went into business together.

...motorbikes

In 1885, German engineer Gottlieb Daimler attached an engine to a wooden bicycle to make the first (rather wobbly) motorbike.

...planes

The Wright brothers made the first powered flight in America in 1903. Their plane only stayed in the air for 12 seconds and, when it landed, the wind blew it away – so they had to build a new one.

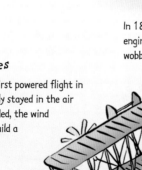

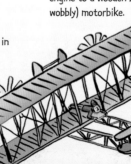

...computers

One of the first computers, the ENIAC, was designed by two American scientists, John Mauchly and J. Presper Eckert. It took them three years to build it. When they finished, in 1946, it took up the space of about five classrooms. The first home computer wasn't invented until 1975 – until then, computers were too big to have at home.

...televisions

The first television was built in 1925 by Scottish inventor John Logie Baird. He made it in his attic out of household objects. By 1929, the British Broadcasting Corporation was using his television system to broadcast tv shows.

...microwave ovens

In 1945, American scientist Percy Spencer was walking past a machine called a magnetron when the chocolate bar in his pocket suddenly melted. He worked out that a kind of energy called microwave energy, emitted by the magnetron, was responsible. He used the magnetron to invent the microwave oven.

...World Wide Web.

In 1989, British scientist Tim Berners-Lee invented a way of sharing information between computers quickly and easily. It's called the World Wide Web, and today it links computers all over the world.

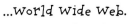

WWW.USBORNE.CO.UK

...MP3 players

The MP3 data storage file was developed by a team of German and US engineers. An MP3 is a type of computer file that contains a digital version of a song or a video.

The first MP3s were released on the internet in 1994, but the first MP3 *players* weren't sold until 1998.

Who knows what could be next?

As physicists make new discoveries, things that seem impossible today might one day become reality. In the future we might zoom through the air on rocket-propelled skateboards, or take a trip to the Moon for a holiday, in our own personal spaceships. Whenever you hear about an amazing new gadget, just think – it's probably thanks to physics.

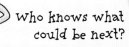

Is the Universe growing or shrinking?

What's an atom and why is it so important?

What are the tiniest things in the Universe?

In what way are these people the same age?

How did an exploding star turn into our Solar System?

Part 1:
The beginning of everything

Physics starts at the very beginning – of everything.
Before the Universe, nothing existed. At all. There was no
sound, or light, or dark. Time and space didn't exist either.
So how did everything come to be
– and what's it all made of?

Read on to find out about the birth of our Universe, and
the tiny bits of stuff that make up *everything* in it...

How did the Universe begin?

Scientists are still struggling to understand how the Universe began. No one knows exactly when or why it started. But in the 1940s physicists came up with a theory known as the **Big Bang**. It goes a bit like this:

The Big Bang

Up until about 13.7 billion years ago, there was nothing. Then suddenly – BANG – there was something. Scientists still don't know how something came out of nothing, but it did. And that something was an incredibly tiny speck.

This speck was really, amazingly small – thousands of times smaller than the head of a pin – but it contained all the matter and energy that has ever existed. The speck exploded, and expanded at an incredible speed.

Within a second it had become a huge, blisteringly hot fireball, and it grew bigger with every moment.

As the fireball spread out, it cooled down and lumps of matter started to form. After about a billion years, these lumps joined together to form the first stars.

Creation ideas

Over the centuries, non-physicists have come up with other ideas for how the Universe might have begun...

An ancient Chinese myth says it all started when a giant hatched from a huge egg. The egg became the heavens and the Earth, and the giant's eyes turned into the Sun and Moon.

An African myth tells how a giant called Mbobo felt a terrible pain in his stomach, and vomited up the Sun, Moon, stars and everything in the world.

In 1975, a French racing car driver called Claude Vorilhon founded a religious cult called Raëlism. His followers believe that aliens used their superior technology to create life on Earth – including humans.

The Big Silence

Although scientists call this event the Big Bang, the beginning of the Universe would actually have been completely silent – because sound can't travel through empty space.

How will it all end?

The Universe is still expanding. Some physicists believe it will go on getting bigger and bigger forever. Others think that, eventually, it will collapse back in on itself in a 'Big Crunch' – and disappear completely – until another Big Bang happens.

Another universe, another you

Who's to say ours is the only universe? Some physicists think there are an infinite number of universes, each one slightly different from the others, which are all expanding towards each other.

Eventually, billions of years from now, they might join together to form a single super-universe. If humans are still around, they might even be able to meet their twins from some of those parallel worlds.

You're a star!
(Well, you used to be...)

Our Solar System – the Sun, and the planets which orbit around it – formed almost 10 billion years after the Universe began, when a huge star exploded...

...leaving a cloud of dust and gas.

Gradually, the dust and gas joined together to create the Sun and the planets. And, eventually...

...us.

What does the Universe look like?

The shape of the Universe is still a mystery. Some scientists believe it's round like a ball, but others think it might look more like a tube, or a giant doughnut.

What's everything made of?

Everything in the Universe, from faraway stars to the ground under your feet, is made from stupendously tiny pieces called **atoms**. Atoms are all so tiny, it's impossible to see them without powerful equipment. The full stop at the end of this sentence contains about 200 million atoms.

Sticking together

Atoms hardly ever float about on their own. They usually join together in clusters to make **molecules**. Every substance there is is made up of atoms or, more often, molecules.

Substances which are made of just one kind of atom, and can't be broken down into simpler substances, are called **elements**. 118 different kinds of atoms have been discovered so far, which means there are 118 elements. Carbon, iron, aluminium and gold are just a few examples.

If you could zoom in on the tip of a pencil a few million times, you would see rows and rows of carbon atoms. There are about 5 million at the tip of a really sharp pencil.

You're as old as your Dad...

Physicists believe all the atoms in the Universe were created at the same instant, in the Big Bang. That means that your atoms are the same age as dinosaur bones – and a new-born baby, and anything else you can think of.

How old are you?

Same as you.

Ooooh, me too.

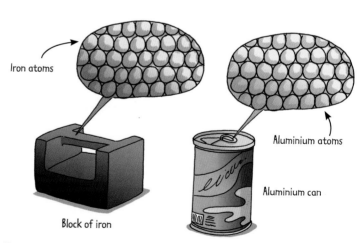

Iron atoms

Aluminium atoms

Aluminium can

Block of iron

But *most* substances contain molecules made of different types of atoms. For example, water molecules are made of hydrogen and oxygen atoms joined together.

Smaller and smaller

By the end of the 19th century, physicists realised that atoms weren't the smallest things in existence – they're made of even tinier particles. They imagined these scattered randomly throughout an atom like fruit in a cake. This was known as the 'plum pudding model'.

In 1909, a scientist named Ernest Rutherford decided to test this model by firing tiny helium atoms, also known as alpha particles, at a thin sheet of gold foil. He expected them to pass through the gold foil in a straight line, or to veer sideways slightly, as if they had hit some 'fruit' (smaller particles).

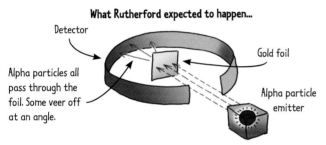

What Rutherford expected to happen...

Detector

Gold foil

Alpha particles all pass through the foil. Some veer off at an angle.

Alpha particle emitter

But, in fact, a few of the alpha particles *bounced back*. It was as if they'd hit one tightly-packed area of matter in the middle of the atom.

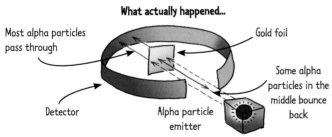

What actually happened...

Most alpha particles pass through

Gold foil

Some alpha particles in the middle bounce back

Detector

Alpha particle emitter

Rutherford was astonished. He said it was as incredible as if he'd fired a bullet at a piece of tissue paper and it had come back to hit him. Turn the page to find out what he discovered...

Turn the page to find out what he discovered...

An ancient idea

The idea of the atom began in Ancient Greece. Philosophers debated what would happen if they cut a substance in half, over and over again. Would they be able to carry on forever? Or would they find something they couldn't cut?

A philosopher called Democritus believed everything was made from indivisible units. He called them *atoma* – meaning 'uncuttable' in Ancient Greek.

Fantastic physicist: Ernest Rutherford 1871-1937

Ernest Rutherford's work earned him a Nobel Prize in 1908 – for chemistry. He was rather taken aback as he was a physicist, not a chemist.

But he decided it didn't matter. He thought that chemistry was just a branch of physics, which he described as "the only real science".

Little and large

All atoms are tiny, but some are tinier than others, because they don't have as many bits.

The very smallest atom is hydrogen, which has just one electron orbiting its nucleus.

The biggest atoms have over 100 electrons.

What's inside an atom?

The structure of an atom is a bit like a miniature solar system. In the middle is a solid part that Rutherford detected, which is now called the **nucleus**.

The nucleus is made from tiny particles known as **protons** and **neutrons**, squashed together in a ball. Even smaller particles called **electrons** zoom around the nucleus – like speeded-up planets orbiting a sun.

This is a model of an atom. The lines show the way electrons move around the nucleus.

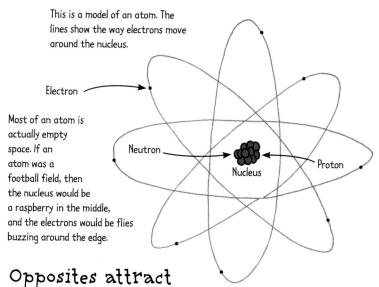

Electron

Neutron

Proton

Nucleus

Most of an atom is actually empty space. If an atom was a football field, then the nucleus would be a raspberry in the middle, and the electrons would be flies buzzing around the edge.

Why can't we walk through things?

If everything is mostly empty space, you might wonder why we can't walk through lamp posts and other things.

While protons and electrons attract each other, two sets of electrons repel each other.

So, when the electrons on the edge of your forehead meet the electrons on the edge of a lamp post, they push each other away.

Stupid electrons!

Opposites attract

Atoms hold together because the different particles are attracted to each other. Have you ever heard the phrase 'opposites attract'? That's definitely true of atomic particles. Protons have a **positive charge** and electrons have a **negative charge**. The reason atoms don't fall apart is because opposite charges attract.

An atom of any element has the same number of protons and electrons, and neutrons don't have any charge of their own. So, overall, the atom is **neutral** – it has neither a positive nor a negative charge.

The smallest things of all?

Until about 50 years ago, scientists thought protons, neutrons and electrons were the smallest bits of matter in existence. But then physicists found a way to break protons and neutrons into even tinier pieces. They did this by smashing them together at incredibly high speeds, inside a machine called a particle accelerator.

Scientists now know that protons and neutrons are made from mind-bogglingly mini specks called **quarks,** which are glued together by even tinier specks called **gluons.**

Inside a particle accelerator

Protons hurtle towards each other...

...and after they've collided, quarks fly out.

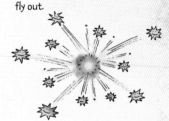

To be continued...

The quest to find the smallest particle is still going on. Physicists spent twenty years building a particle accelerator in Switzerland, the Large Hadron Collider (LHC), to look for one tiny piece of matter they weren't even sure existed. They named it anyway, though: the Higgs boson.

Inside the LHC

Scientists think the Higgs boson existed for a fraction of a second after the Big Bang, so they're using the LHC to recreate the Big Bang in miniature, to try to find it.

About the Large Hadron Collider

● Building the LHC to recreate the Big Bang was the largest scientific endeavour ever conducted.

● If it weren't for the LHC, the World Wide Web might not exist. Tim Berners-Lee created the Web so scientists all over the world could share information more quickly, to help with the design of the LHC.

● The Higgs boson — if it really exists — is so important that some scientists have nicknamed it the 'God particle'.

● Some scientists feared the LHC would create giant black holes which would swallow up the Earth when it was first switched on in 2008 — but that didn't happen.

● The LHC was only switched on for 10 days — not long enough to find the Higgs boson.

Part 2:
Feel the force

A force is a push or a pull. You can't see a force, but you can see what it does. Forces can get things moving, or make them change direction. They can speed things up and slow them down, too. Forces can squeeze things, or change their shape. But, whatever they do, forces always act in a straight line.

Forces act on all of us all the time. Often forces balance and cancel each other out, so you don't notice them. But when they don't balance, they become more obvious. Read on to find out about different kinds of forces and what they do.

Speed and motion

Speed triangle

Physics is full of word equations that describe how to calculate one measurement if you know two others. Most of them can be drawn up in a 'magic triangle':

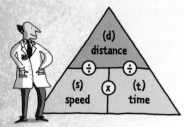

If you cover up the measurement you're trying to work out, you'll be left with the equation you need.

To find out the quantity at the top, you multiply the two at the bottom. So:

d = s x t

If you need to work out either of the quantities at the bottom, you divide the top by the other bottom quantity. So:

$$s = \frac{d}{t} \quad \text{and} \quad t = \frac{d}{s}$$

Imagine you're pushing a trolley in a supermarket. That push is a force. The result of the force is that the trolley moves. If you push harder – in other words, apply a greater force – the trolley will move faster. Its **speed** will increase. But exactly how fast is the trolley moving? And how fast are you moving yourself?

Speed is a measure of the *distance* something travels in a certain *time*. Physicists measure speed in metres per second (m/s) – how many metres something travels in a second. You can work speed out using this formula:

$$\text{speed (s)} = \frac{\text{distance (d)}}{\text{time (t)}}$$

These people in a supermarket are all moving at different speeds:

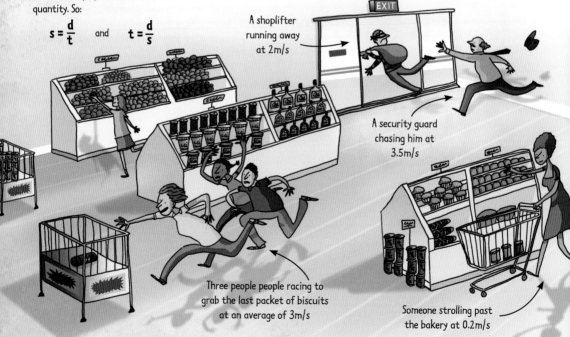

A shoplifter running away at 2m/s

A security guard chasing him at 3.5m/s

Three people people racing to grab the last packet of biscuits at an average of 3m/s

Someone strolling past the bakery at 0.2m/s

Now imagine you're in the supermarket too and YOU want the last packet of biscuits. You skid 12 metres down the aisle and reach it in 3 seconds. To work out your speed, you divide the distance you travelled by the time it took:

$$\text{speed} = \frac{\text{distance}}{\text{time}} = \frac{12 \text{ metres}}{3 \text{ seconds}} = 4\text{m/s}$$

This means you were travelling at 4 metres per second. That's faster than anyone else in the supermarket.

which way?

The thing about forces is that they always act in a straight line. Physicists use the word **velocity (v)** to describe how fast something is moving in a particular direction. Like speed, it's measured in m/s.

Something can change velocity by changing direction, even if it doesn't change speed. It can also change velocity by speeding up (or accelerating) or slowing down (or decelerating).

Acceleration and **deceleration** are measured in metres per second *per second*, which is written m/s² (how much velocity changes in a second).

You can work out acceleration using this formula:

$$\text{acceleration} = \frac{\textbf{end velocity – start velocity}}{\textbf{time}}$$

Suppose, trying to outrun the security guard, the shoplifter runs faster, increasing his velocity from 0 m/s to 4 m/s in 5 seconds (without changing direction).

$$\text{Acceleration} = \frac{4-0 \text{ metres/second}}{5 \text{ seconds}} = \frac{4}{5} = 0.8\text{m/s}^2$$

So the shoplifter's acceleration is 0.8 metres per second per second in the direction of the exit.

m/s or km/h?

On a motorway, a car can easily travel about 33 metres in a second. But because a car can travel very fast for a long time, people usually talk about how many *kilometres* (km) it can travel in an *hour* (h).

Divide by 1,000 to convert metres into kilometres: 33m = 0.033km

Multiply by 60 to convert seconds into minutes, and by 60 again to convert minutes into hours. 0.033 x 60 x 60 = 118.8

33m/s is the same as 118.8km/h.

Slowing down

You can work out deceleration in almost the same way as acceleration.

This is the formula:

$$\textbf{deceleration} = \frac{\textbf{start velocity – end velocity}}{\textbf{time}}$$

When the security guard catches him, the shoplifter slows down from 4m/s to 0m/s in 10 seconds. What's his deceleration?

$$\text{Deceleration} = \frac{4-0}{10} = \frac{4}{10}$$

$$\text{Deceleration} = 0.4\text{m/s}^2$$

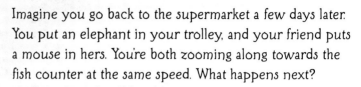

Mass matters

Why roads have speed limits

When a car is driving really fast, it has a lot of momentum. This makes it hard to slow down and stop, even if the car has really good brakes.

A car that's driving above the speed limit will take longer to stop, and will do much more damage if it crashes, than a car driving at the limit.

Imagine you go back to the supermarket a few days later. You put an elephant in your trolley, and your friend puts a mouse in hers. You're both zooming along towards the fish counter at the same speed. What happens next?

Your friend will be able to stop her trolley neatly at the counter. But you will find it incredibly hard to steer and stop – so your trolley will smash into the counter, showering seafood everywhere.

But *why*? Well, it's because the elephant in your trolley is so *massive*. The original meaning of 'massive' is something that has a lot of **mass** – or in other words, contains a lot of **matter**, or stuff. When something with a lot of mass is moving at a high velocity, it also has a lot of something called momentum.

What's momentum?

Momentum is a measure of how *forcefully* something is moving in a particular direction. If something has a lot of mass (such as an elephant), it's hard to start it moving, because the amount of mass weighs it down.

But once it *is* moving, that mass and the velocity it's moving at make it even harder to slow down, or steer, than it was to get it going in the first place.

The greater the mass of an object, and the higher its velocity, the more momentum it has. Of course, physicists like to know *exactly* how much momentum an object has.

Massively different

Because a mouse has so much less mass than an elephant, the only way they could have the same *momentum* is if the elephant was walking really slowly, and the mouse was zooming along almost as fast as light – which is the fastest thing in the Universe.

LIGHT SPEED ROCKET

20

Mass is measured in kilograms, and velocity in metres per second, so momentum is measured in kilogram metres per second (kg m/s).

momentum (p) = mass (m) x velocity (v)

Where does force come into it?

It takes force to make the trolley (and the elephant) move in the first place. And it takes force to make it stop. You might be strong enough to get the trolley going, but it would probably take a weightlifter to stop the trolley crashing. The trolley's momentum would be so great, only a weightlifter could exert a big enough force to stop it.

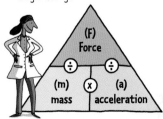

Force (F) is measured in kg m/s², more simply called **newtons (N)**, and can be calculated using this formula:

Force (F) = mass (m) x acceleration (a)

If the elephant in the trolley had a mass of 6,000kg, and was accelerating towards the fish counter at 0.2m/s², what would be the force exerted on the counter?

Force = mass x acceleration

= 6,000kg x 0.2m/s² = 1200N

So to stop the crash, the weightlifter would have to pull on the trolley with an equivalent force of 1200 newtons.

Momentum triangle

Here's another magic triangle you can use to work out momentum, mass and velocity. It looks like this:

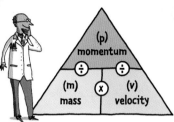

Measuring force

The strength of a force can be measured with a **force meter**.

This device contains a spring attached to a hook. When you apply a force to the hook, the spring stretches. You can read the size of the force in newtons down the side.

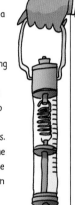

Force triangle

Force, mass and acceleration can be worked out using this magic triangle:

Different kinds of forces

The force you use to get a trolley going is an example of a 'push' force.

If you wanted to open a cupboard door, you'd use a pull force.

Here are some of the main kinds of forces...

...push & pull

Most forces are pushes or pulls of some kind.

...elastic

Elastic force makes something bounce back when you've stretched it – like elastic.

SQUEAK!!!

...compression

Compression is the force you exert when you squash something.

...twist

When you turn a door handle or twist the lid of a jar, you're using a twisting force.

...electrical

Electrical force is caused by charged particles attracting or repelling each other. Static electricity is an example of electrical force. This is what makes your hair stand on end when it's rubbed by a balloon.

...magnetic

This is the force that makes magnets attract or repel each other.

...tension

Tension is the force that things have when they're pulled tight, like a rope in a tug-of-war.

Friction — there's the rub

Now imagine you're back in the supermarket. You give the trolley a big push and let it go, sending it wheeling along the aisle. Eventually, the trolley will naturally slow down and stop. This is because of friction.

Friction is a force which happens when two things rub together, like the wheels and the floor. It opposes motion and makes things slow down.

If you took the trolley outside and tried to wheel it across grass, you would have to push much harder. The rough grass would catch against the wheels more than the smooth floor, increasing friction and slowing down the trolley.

Sometimes friction can be a real hindrance, but it can be a great help, too...

Defeating friction

Friction between two things can be reduced if they are separated with a thin layer of liquid, or lubricant.

If you've ever seen anyone fixing a car engine, you'll know they often end up with grease all over their hands. The grease helps the engine parts to move over each other smoothly.

Without friction, you wouldn't be able to tie your shoelaces. They'd be so slippery, they'd slide off each other.

AHHHH!

Brakes wouldn't work without friction, so there would be a lot more accidents.

Have you ever been annoyed by a creaky door or a squeaky wheel? It's friction between the moving parts that causes the sound.

If there wasn't any friction, you'd slide all over the place and wouldn't be able to stand up...

...but you'd never graze your knees when you fell over.

SQUEAK

It's the law!

Over 300 years ago, Isaac Newton studied forces and came up with a set of laws to explain how things move. These laws apply just as much to the latest sports car as to the first ball that was ever kicked across the ground. They're known as **Newton's Laws of Motion**.

Don't change – the first law

Newton's first observation was that *an object which isn't moving won't start moving unless a force is applied to it*. A football lying on the ground won't score a goal on its own – someone has to kick it.

She kicked it!

I never touched it!

Ah, but you must have. An object at rest will stay at rest unless an unbalanced force acts on it.

This seems pretty obvious. But the first law also states that, *once an object is moving, it won't stop unless another force makes it stop*.

So the football will carry on sailing through the air unless it hits the back of the net, or the goalkeeper catches it, or the Earth's gravity drags it down (see page 30) and friction stops it rolling across the grass.

In other words, *objects resist changing velocity – they won't speed up, slow down or change direction on their own*. This is called **inertia**.

Fantastic physicist: Isaac Newton 1642–1727

Isaac Newton was one of the most influential scientists ever. He explained gravity, invented a whole new form of maths, known as calculus, and came up with the laws of motion. Newtons, the units that force is measured in, are named after him.

Before Newton's work on forces, many people still believed in a theory of motion developed by Aristotle, an Ancient Greek philosopher.

Aristotle believed substances made of different things moved in different ways. He thought stones fell towards Earth because they were made of earth, and smoke rose into the sky because it was mostly made of air.

Egg-nertia

Liquids have inertia (see right) too. Spin a raw egg on a plate. Stop it spinning with your fingers, then let go almost immediately. It should start spinning again, because the runny egg inside the shell won't have stopped moving.

Defining a force — the second law

Newton's second law defines what a force is, and says that *the force needed to change something's velocity depends on its mass.* That's really just another way of saying **force = mass x acceleration**.

If you give a shopping trolley with a mouse in it a little push, it will move across the floor. But it will get moving much faster if you give it a bigger push. *Things accelerate more quickly if the force pushing them is greater.*

You'd have to give the trolley with the elephant a much bigger push to get it moving at the same speed. In other words, *the larger an object is, the greater the force needed to make it accelerate the same amount.*

The bigger the force, the more something will accelerate. The more mass something has, the bigger the force needed to make it accelerate.

Unscary equation

This is how to work out the force needed to make an elephant with a mass of 700kg accelerate at 5m/s^2:

F = m x a   F = 700 x 5
F = 3500N

So what force would you need to make a 0.05kg mouse accelerate at the same speed?

A push and a pull — the third law

Newton's third law states that *whenever there is a force acting on something in one direction, another force of the same size is acting on it in the opposite direction.*

The first two laws are pretty obvious, but this one can *seem* surprising. After all, when you push a trolley, it doesn't push you back – or does it?

Imagine you're getting out of a boat. As you step out, the force from your legs pushes the boat down into the water and away from you. It's the boat *pushing back* that gives you the force to step up onto dry land. Of course, if you don't tie the boat to the dock first, your legs will push the boat too far away and you might fall in...

I keep telling you: for every action there is an equal and opposite reaction.

work harder!

work triangle

Here's a magic triangle to show how to calculate work, force and distance from each other:

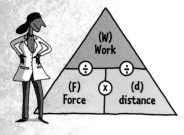

According to the laws of physics, when you use a force to move something you're doing **work**. The bigger the force, or the further you move an object, the more work you do.

So in physics, you actually do more work when you pick up a chocolate bar and eat it than when you solve a problem in a physics book.

As well as defining what work is, physicists have also come up with a way to measure amounts of work. They use **joules (J)**, which are also called newton metres (Nm). You can calculate the amount of work done using this formula:

Work (W) = Force (F) x distance (d)

Unscary equations

How much work do you do when you use a force of 0.5N to lift a pen 40cm (0.4m) to scratch your head?

See if you were right below.

Imagine you've had enough of that massive elephant you've been carting around. You want him to go back to the zoo, but he doesn't want to leave, so you have to push him all the way.

You'd need to use a force of 400N and the zoo is 100m away.

How much work would you have to do?

Work = force x distance = 400N x 100m = 40,000J

You'd need to do 40,000 joules of work – which is very difficult, even for the world's strongest weightlifter. But do not despair! Read on to find out how physics can help...

ZOO

Physics makes work easier

Since it's too hard to *push* your elephant to the zoo, you could try *wheeling* him there in a shopping trolley. It would be easier than just pushing him, because a trolley is a kind of machine.

In physics, a **machine** is something that makes it easier to do work. Most people use lots of machines every day without realizing it.

Here are some very simple machines. You'll see machines everywhere once you start to look.

Fulcrum

Lever

A lever is something that has a fixed point, called a **fulcrum**, which stays still while other parts move. It converts a weak force you exert over a long distance into a strong force over a short distance on the other side of the fulcrum.

Pliers, bottle-openers and shoehorns are all kinds of lever.

Inclined plane

An inclined plane is a sloped surface. It's much easier to move something up an inclined plane than lifting it straight up, just as it's easier to wander along a sloping path than drag yourself up a cliff face.

Wheel

The wheel is one of the simplest machines of all. It's easier to transport things using wheels because they turn, rather than just dragging across the ground. This reduces the impact of friction.

Pulley

A pulley is a wheel with a rope attached. It turns a weak force over a long distance into a strong force over a short distance, a bit like a lever. But unlike a lever, a pulley changes the direction of your force. A set of pulleys would help you hoist an elephant *up*, even though you're pulling the rope *down*.

Wedge

A wedge is a kind of inclined plane. Some wedges, like axes and shovels, are used to break things apart. Others, like doorstops, stop things moving.

Screw

A screw is a curved inclined plane. Screws are useful for holding things together. If you screw a shelf to a wall, it's unlikely to fall off.

27

Gravity — it makes you more attractive

Newton and the apple

Isaac Newton didn't discover the force of gravity – but he was the first person to explain what it is.

The story goes that an apple fell from a tree and hit him on the head, and he guessed a force was pulling it towards the Earth.

Gravity is a force which pulls objects together. If you drop something, gravity makes it fall to the ground. Without gravity, it would just hang in the air.

Everything that has mass has gravity too, but you only notice the gravity of *really* massive objects, like the Sun, the Earth or other planets, which pull everything towards them.

Gravity in space is almost non-existent. You might have seen videos of astronauts in spaceships spinning around and chasing after floating objects. If it wasn't for the Earth's gravity pulling us down, we'd float around all the time, too.

Space to grow

Astronauts grow taller in space because there is almost no gravity pushing the discs in their spines together. But they shrink down to normal when they get back to Earth.

Gravity

No gravity

Likewise, if the Moon wasn't attracted by the Earth's gravity, it would drift off into space instead of circling the Earth. The Moon's gravity also affects the Earth — it pulls the seas and oceans, causing the tides.

How much do you weigh?

On the Earth's surface, the pull of gravity makes everything accelerate downwards at about $10m/s^2$. This is what gives you your **weight** – weight is actually the force Earth's gravity exerts on you. In physics, weight is measured in newtons. A set of 'weighing' scales is really measuring mass (in kg).

To work out your weight on Earth, you need to multiply your mass by the amount Earth's gravity makes you accelerate ($10m/s^2$).

A mass-ive difference

Mass is the amount of matter in an object. It is constant (doesn't ever change).

Weight measures how strongly gravity pulls on an object. It is a force that changes depending on where the object is.

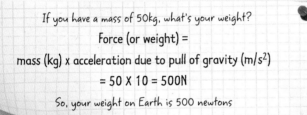

If you have a mass of 50kg, what's your weight?

Force (or weight) =

mass (kg) x acceleration due to pull of gravity (m/s^2)

$$= 50 \times 10 = 500N$$

So, your weight on Earth is 500 newtons

How to lose weight quickly

If you climbed to the top of a really tall building you'd weigh a tiny bit less than you did at ground level – but you wouldn't be any thinner. Your *mass* wouldn't change, but your *weight* would, because gravity gets weaker with distance. It pulls on you less as you move further away from the centre of the Earth.

On Earth, it's hard to climb high enough for your weight to change dramatically. But if you went to the Moon, you'd weigh six times less.

The Moon is so much smaller than Earth, it only has one sixth of the Earth's gravity. So you'd be able to jump six times as high – and kick a ball much further, too.

What would you weigh on different planets?

If you weighed 500N on earth, you'd weigh...

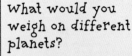

...89N on Mars (a small planet, with low gravity)...

...and 1182N on Jupiter (a huge planet, with high gravity).

Forces: a matter of life and death

What if there's no air?

Without air resistance, everything would fall at exactly the same rate of acceleration, regardless of size or mass.

In 1971, an astronaut decided to test this by dropping a hammer and a feather on the Moon. Because the Moon has no air resistance, they fell at the same rate and landed at the same time.

The further things fall, the more chance the force of gravity has to make them accelerate. If someone next to you dropped a penny on your head, it wouldn't hurt very much. But if he dropped it from the top of a skyscraper, by the time it hit you it'd be moving about as fast as a speeding bullet, and might badly injure you.

Falling things don't keep getting faster forever. As the penny falls, air rubs against it and slows it down. This is called **air resistance**, and it's a form of friction.

Eventually, the air resistance would be equal to the falling force (or weight) of the penny, so it would stop accelerating and fall at a constant speed. This natural speed limit is called **terminal velocity**.

If you jumped out of an aeroplane without a parachute, you'd accelerate downwards until you reached a terminal velocity of about 59m/s – so fast, you'd die when you hit the ground. But if you had a parachute, the air would have a greater area to push against. This extra air resistance would slow your terminal velocity to about 5.4m/s, so you'd land gently.

Resisting resistance

Air resistance can be really useful, as parachutes prove. But sometimes, people don't want air to slow them down.

Fast-moving jet planes are smooth and streamlined, with pointy tips, so the air doesn't have much area to push against.

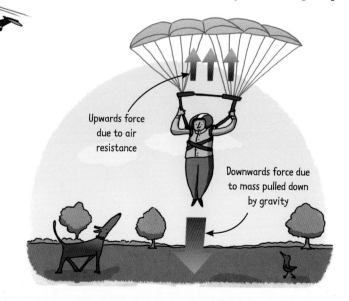

Upwards force due to air resistance

Downwards force due to mass pulled down by gravity

Going around in circles

If things move because of forces, and forces always act in a straight line, how can things move in *circles*? Well, they can do this because of **centripetal force**, a force which pulls all spinning things towards the middle of a circle.

Imagine you're a cowboy spinning a lasso. Your hand is exerting a centripetal force on it, pulling it inwards. As the lasso spins, its velocity is constantly changing direction, making the lasso move in a circle, even though the force itself is acting in a straight line. Without a centripetal force, it wouldn't go around in a circle. So when you let go (to catch a cow, or a bandit), the lasso flies off in a straight line.

See for yourself: centripetal force

Try spinning a scarf like a lasso. Your hand provides a centripetal force, which pulls the scarf in towards your hand.

If you let go of it, the scarf will carry on moving in a straight line, until gravity pulls it down.

Spinning the lasso...

...and letting it go.

If you've ridden on a fast-spinning funfair ride, you might have felt as if you were being pulled outwards, away from the middle of the ride. What you're actually feeling is inertia – your body resisting the constant centripetal force that the ride is exerting on you.

Because you're moving around in a circle, you feel the effects of inertia constantly – because you're always changing direction. This inertia is described as **centrifugal 'force'**, although it isn't really a force at all.

See for yourself: centrifugal force

Hold hands with a friend and spin around in a circle. You might notice that your hair flies out behind you and you feel as if you're being pulled outwards.

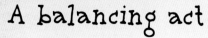

A balancing act

Because gravity is always pulling us down, staying upright isn't always easy. Just try balancing on one leg and see how long you can stay like that.

Balancing is all about something physicists call the **centre of gravity**.

What's the centre of gravity?

The Earth's gravity pulls down on every particle in an object (such as your body) with a force related to that object's mass. Although the force pulls on every particle, the combined effect of all the forces appears to pull down on just one imaginary point, which physicists have named 'the centre of gravity'.

Every object that has weight has a centre of gravity. As long as that centre is over the base of the object, it will be stable. But sometimes, the centre of gravity can end up hanging away from the base.

Imagine a (mean) person gave you a push. If you were standing firmly on two legs, you wouldn't budge. But now imagine you're wearing a backpack full of camping gear. Your centre of gravity would be behind you, and you probably *would* fall over.

Balletic balancing

Ballet dancers spend quite a lot of time standing on one foot. They also make a lot of beautiful shapes with their arms.

These arm movements aren't just decorative – they help the dancers to balance, by altering their centre of gravity.

Lifting a ladder

If you tried to pick up a ladder at one end, you'd be really far away from its centre of gravity and it would be hard to lift the whole ladder off the ground.

But if you hold the ladder in the middle, it's much easier to pick it up.

Centre of gravity

Base

Centre of gravity

Base

Keeping upright

It's very hard to make something fall over if it has a low centre of gravity. That's because you'd have to tip it quite far to make its centre move away from its base. Here are some examples...

The Leaning Tower of Pisa

The Leaning Tower of Pisa famously leans quite a lot. Scientists were worried it might eventually fall over. So they added extra mass to the bottom of the tower to lower its centre of gravity.

They could have tried to straighten it – but then it would just have been an ordinary tower.

Sumo wrestlers usually squat when they're preparing to fight each other. This makes it harder for their opponents to push them over.

Racing cars are built low to the ground, to stop them tipping over when they drive around tight corners.

Surfers crouch low over their surfboards and wave their arms about a lot to keep their balance.

See for yourself: centre of gravity

Try pushing over an empty plastic bottle. It should be pretty easy to make it topple over.

Centre of gravity

Try again with the bottle half-full of water. It should be harder to topple because the water makes the bottle heavier at the bottom, so it has a lower centre of gravity.

Centre of gravity

Now fill the bottle to the top with water. It'll be easier to topple again. Because the water fills the whole bottle, the weight is spread out and its centre of gravity will be higher again.

Centre of gravity

Under pressure

A force can be applied to a small area or a large area with different effects. Try pushing your thumb into a piece of wood. You probably won't even make a dent. But if you push down with the same force on a drawing pin, it will go deep into the wood.

That's because your push is now concentrated over a smaller area (the end of the pin), which means the *pressure* applied to the wood is greater.

Pressure is the amount of force there is on something over a certain area. It's measured in newtons per square metre (N/m^2), sometimes known as pascals (Pa). The formula for working it out is:

$$\text{Pressure (P)} = \frac{\text{Force (F)}}{\text{Area (A)}}$$

How can a magician lie on a bed of nails?

Some magicians wow their audiences by lying on a bed of nails. It might look painful, but it doesn't hurt that much, as long as there are enough nails to spread their weight.

If a magician only lay on one nail, his body would exert a lot of pressure on it – and he'd get a nasty nail-shaped hole in his back.

How much pressure do you apply with your thumb, if you push with a force of 2N, and the area of your thumb is $2cm^2$ ($0.0002m^2$)?

$$\text{Pressure} = \frac{\text{force}}{\text{area}} = \frac{2N}{0.0002m^2} = 10,000N/m^2$$

$10,000N/m^2$ is the same as just $10N/cm^2$ – so your thumb isn't applying that much pressure.

Now, how much pressure do you apply with the drawing pin, if the force you use is still 2N, and the tip of the pin has an area of half a square millimetre ($0.0000005m^2$)?

$$\text{Pressure} = \frac{\text{force}}{\text{area}} = \frac{2N}{0.0000005m^2} = 4,000,000N/m^2$$

The pin applies four million newtons per square metre of pressure, or the same as $4,000N/cm^2$ – 400 times as much pressure as you apply with your thumb.

Why pressure makes you bleed

It's not just solids that apply pressure to other things. Liquids always push against the sides of whatever container they're in, trying to escape.

This includes the blood inside you. Your heart pumps blood around your body. The blood is constantly pushing outwards, but your veins and arteries hold it in. If you cut yourself, it can escape through the hole – and you bleed.

Gases exert pressure, too. The air in the atmosphere pushes on us with enormous pressure. Luckily, the liquid inside our bodies pushes back with equal pressure. Otherwise, we'd be squashed to death by the weight of the air.

See for yourself: pressure

Use a pair of scissors to make two holes in the side of an empty aluminium drinks can, one near the top and one near the bottom. Cover the holes with sticky tape, and fill the can with water.

Stand the can by a sink, and pull off the tape.

You should find water spurts out further from the lower hole because it's under more pressure, caused by the weight of the water above it.

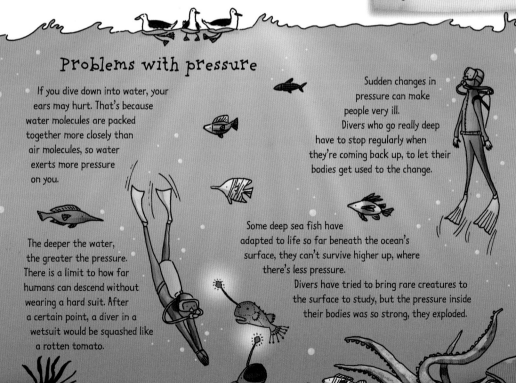

Problems with pressure

If you dive down into water, your ears may hurt. That's because water molecules are packed together more closely than air molecules, so water exerts more pressure on you.

The deeper the water, the greater the pressure. There is a limit to how far humans can descend without wearing a hard suit. After a certain point, a diver in a wetsuit would be squashed like a rotten tomato.

Sudden changes in pressure can make people very ill.
Divers who go really deep have to stop regularly when they're coming back up, to let their bodies get used to the change.

Some deep sea fish have adapted to life so far beneath the ocean's surface, they can't survive higher up, where there's less pressure.
Divers have tried to bring rare creatures to the surface to study, but the pressure inside their bodies was so strong, they exploded.

Why does wood float?

Measuring volume

Volume is measured in cubic metres (m^3). If you want to measure the volume of a box, for example, you multiply its length by its width by its height.

If you drop a stone into a river, it'll sink. If you drop a piece of wood, it'll float. The force of gravity acting on the wood and the stone is the same, so why does one thing float and not the other?

It's all because of something called **density**. Density describes how much mass is packed into an object. A stone is denser than water, so it sinks. Wood is less dense than water, so it floats.

You can work out the exact density of an object by comparing its mass to its **volume** (how much space it takes up). Volume is measured in cubic metres (m^3), and density is measured in kilograms per cubic metre (kg/m^3). Here's a handy formula for calculating density:

$$\text{density } (\varrho) = \frac{\text{mass } (m)}{\text{Volume } (V)}$$

Density triangle

Here's another magic triangle to help you work out density, mass and volume.

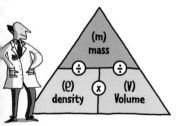

The symbol for 'density' might look a bit strange. It was tricky for physicists because 'd' already stands for distance. So they borrowed the Greek letter 'ϱ' (pronounced 'rho') instead.

Lighter than air

Imagine you have a dolphin-shaped helium balloon on the end of a string, exactly the same size and shape as a real dolphin. If you let it go, the balloon would float in the air – but there's no way that a real dolphin would.

It's all because of density:

Real dolphin's mass = 160kg   Real dolphin's volume = $2m^3$

Real dolphin's density $= \dfrac{m}{V} = \dfrac{160kg}{2m^3} = 80kg/m^3$

Balloon-dolphin's mass = 0.1kg   Balloon-dolphin's volume = $2m^3$

Balloon-dolphin's density $= \dfrac{m}{V} = \dfrac{0.1kg}{2m^3} = 0.05kg/m^3$

The density of air is about 1.2 kilograms per cubic metre. Helium balloons are much less dense than air, so they float. Dolphins are much more dense than air, so they don't float.

Why does a huge steel ship float?

Water has a density of 1,000kg/m³, but steel is much denser (about 9,000kg/m³), so a solid lump of steel will sink. But a ship made of steel isn't a solid lump. Inside there are lots of empty rooms filled with air, which has a low density (1.2kg/m³). Because there is so much air, the ship's *overall* density is less than water's, so it floats.

Submarines use density to dive or float. When the crew want to go underwater, they let sea water fill up empty tanks inside the submarine. This increases the submarine's density, so it sinks. To come up again, they pump air back into the tanks, so the submarine's density decreases.

A submarine floating on the surface.

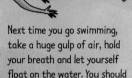

See for yourself: changing density

Next time you go swimming, take a huge gulp of air, hold your breath and let yourself float on the water. You should find it's quite easy.

Then blow the air out again. You should find you sink a little lower, and it gets harder to float. This is because you'll have less air in your lungs, so your average density becomes higher.

An elephant in the bath

Next time you have a bath, look at what happens to the water. Notice how it moves up the sides of the bath when you get in. This is called **displacement**.

The amount of water you push out of the way (or displace) is equal to the volume of your body. If a mouse got into your bath, it wouldn't displace much water. But if an elephant got in, so much water would be displaced there wouldn't be much left in the bath.

Displacement is a useful way of measuring the volume of an object which has an odd shape. You can drop it into a container filled to the brim with water, and collect the water it displaces. The volume of the water displaced will be the same as the volume of the object.

Fantastic physicist: Archimedes about 287–212BC

The first person to notice displacement was Ancient Greek scientist Archimedes. It's said he filled his bath too full, and water splashed out when he got in.

He was so excited by his new idea that he ran into the street naked, shouting "Eureka!" ("I've got it!").

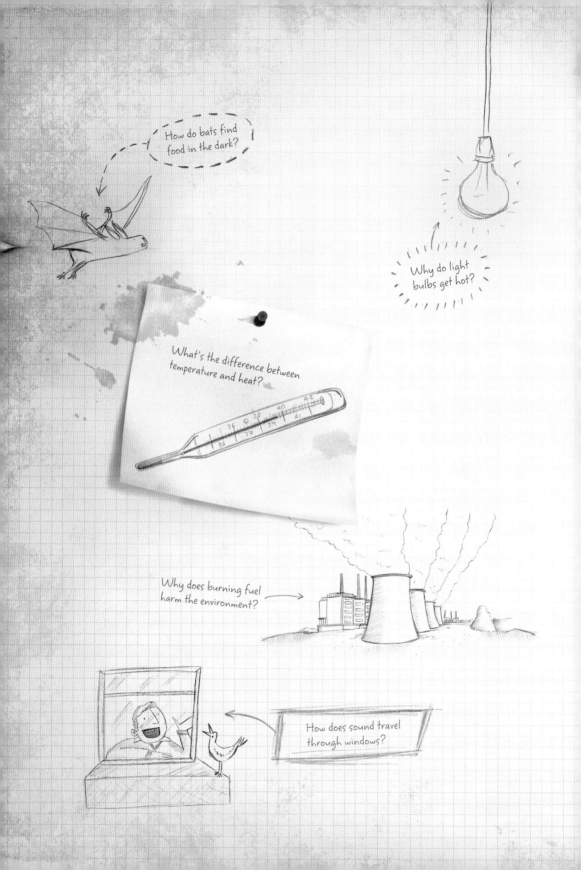

Part 3:
Energy everywhere

If there were no energy, nothing would ever happen.
Like everything else in the Universe, energy was created
in the Big Bang. And now it's everywhere, in everything.

Light energy is what allows you to see this book, and
if someone asks you a question, you can hear it because
of sound energy. If you decide to walk away, you use
movement or 'kinetic' energy. Read on to find out more
about these kinds of energy, and discover how one kind of
energy can change into another.

Why is energy like a superhero?

Kinds of energy

Energy comes in many forms.

Sound energy – energy that you hear.

Heat energy – energy you feel as heat.

Chemical energy – stored energy (e.g. in food, fuel or batteries).

Kinetic energy – movement energy.

Light energy – energy that allows us to see.

Potential energy – energy that something has because of its position (e.g. above the ground, because gravity is pulling on it), or if it's squashed or stretched.

Electrical energy – energy that comes from the movement of electrons. We use it to power our homes.

Magnetic energy – energy that makes magnetic objects, such as magnets, attract or repel each other.

Nuclear energy – energy stored in the nuclei of atoms.

To a physicist, **energy** is the ability to do work – it makes it possible to exert a force and move things.

Energy isn't a physical thing you can touch, in the way you can touch matter. But energy has all sorts of powers to affect things. In fact, you could see energy as the ultimate superhero...

Energy is all-powerful: nothing could move without energy to exert a force.

Energy is everywhere: everything that exists has energy of some kind.

Energy can take many different forms, and change form as if by magic.

Energy is immortal: it's impossible to destroy it. New energy can't be created – all the energy in the Universe has been around since the Big Bang, although it keeps changing from one form to another.

Energy gets things done. The release of energy does work – for example, when you run down the road. And, when work is done on something (on a pencil, if you pick it up, for example), energy is *added* to it.

Where do you get your energy from?

If anyone's ever asked you this question, now you can tell them the *real* answer. All the energy on Earth comes from heat and light from the Sun. When that energy is used, it doesn't disappear: it changes form.

This is known as **energy transfer**. It works like this:

1. THE SUN SENDS OUT HEAT AND LIGHT ENERGY.

2. SEEDS USE HEAT AND LIGHT TO GROW INTO HEALTHY PLANTS.

3. PLANTS PRODUCE FRUITS WHICH STORE THE ENERGY AS CHEMICAL ENERGY.

4. WHEN YOU EAT FRUITS, AND OTHER FOOD, THE CHEMICAL ENERGY IS TRANSFERRED TO YOUR BODY, WHERE IT'S STORED, UNTIL...

5. ...YOU GO OUT TO PLAY, CONVERTING CHEMICAL ENERGY INTO KINETIC ENERGY AND HEAT.

If energy can't be destroyed, why worry about 'saving energy'?

Like all superheroes, energy has a weakness. When it changes form – whether from chemical to kinetic, or electrical to light – some of it always turns into heat. That's why light bulbs, computers and televisions get warm when they're used, and why you get hot if you do a lot of exercise.

Heat is much harder to catch and recycle than other kinds of energy, so most of that heat escapes into the atmosphere. Heat can build up in the atmosphere, warming the whole planet.

The energy to drive

This is how energy changing form can make a car go:

A car is filled with petrol, which contains chemical energy.

Explosion happens in here

Inside the car engine, a spark makes a tiny amount of the petrol explode. The explosion pushes a piston, which turns an axle and makes the wheels spin. Chemical energy from the petrol is converted into kinetic energy. Some is also turned into sound and heat.

Piston

Axle

VROOOM

But where does petrol come from? Turn the page to find out...

Hot topic

Most of the energy we use to heat houses, run computers and make cars go comes from fuels such as oil, coal and natural gas.

These are called **fossil fuels** because they're formed from the fossilized remains of living things — things that died millions of years ago and were squashed together deep under the ground. Coal is made from dead plants, and oil and natural gas from dead sea creatures.

What's the problem with fossil fuels?

One problem is that the Earth is running out of fossil fuels — and it'll be millions of years before new ones form. But scientists have discovered a worse problem: burning fossil fuels is bad for the environment.

When they're burned, fossil fuels give off waste gases. Some of these pollute the air and water, and harm living things. And most of them, including carbon dioxide (CO_2), contribute to **global warming**: an increase in the temperature of the air and oceans.

What's wrong with global warming?

You might think global warming just means more summery weather. But even a tiny rise in temperature causes huge problems around the world. These include:

• Melting icecaps, which lead to colder seas, rising sea levels and flooding in some places.

• More extreme weather, such as hurricanes and droughts, which cause massive damage.

• Changing climates. Some parts of the world may become too hot for many animals, including humans, to live. Some types of animals may even die out entirely.

Power stations convert chemical energy in fossil fuels into electrical energy. But they pollute the environment at the same time.

Where else can we get energy from?

Scientists are still working hard to try to find sources of energy that are both safe *and* efficient. Until they succeed, it's best if everyone reduces the amount of energy they use, so that global warming will be reduced and existing energy sources will last longer.

Here are some of the best alternative energy sources that exist today:

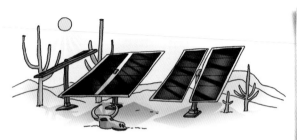

Solar power

How it works: solar panels convert heat from the Sun into electrical energy people can use.

Advantage: doesn't pollute the environment.

Disadvantage: the panels are expensive to build. And they're not very effective on cloudy days.

Wind power

How it works: wind turns the blades of a turbine, which converts kinetic energy into electricity.

Advantage: doesn't pollute the environment with harmful gases.

Disadvantage: can't work if there's no wind, or if there's a really strong wind.

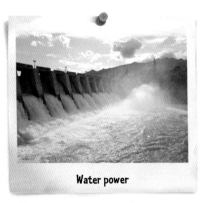

Water power

How it works: converts the kinetic energy from moving water (such as waves or waterfalls) into electricity.

Advantage: even a small water power station can produce lots of energy.

Disadvantage: building a station means building a dam to store the water. This can damage the local environment.

Nuclear power

How it works: produces energy by splitting atoms.

Advantage: produces a large amount of energy without making much CO_2.

Disadvantage: produces toxic nuclear waste, which has to be stored very carefully for thousands of years, until it becomes harmless.

You've got the power

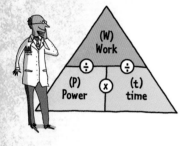
If you're sent upstairs to tidy your room, you might drag your feet, and take as long as possible. But if someone tells you there's a surprise waiting up there, you might rush upstairs pretty quickly. You'll have done the same amount of work, but in much less time – meaning you'll have used more *power* to do it.

Power is a measure of the amount of work done – or the amount of energy converted – in a particular time. Here's a formula to calculate power:

$$\text{Power (P)} = \frac{\text{Work (W)}}{\text{time (t)}}$$

Work is measured in joules, and so power is measured in joules per second (J/s) – the number of joules of energy that are converted every second.

Joules per second are also known as watts (W), so 1 J/s = 1 W.

Light bulb? Watt light bulb?

You might have noticed that the brightness of light bulbs is measured in watts. Usually, the higher the number of watts, the brighter the bulb.

But the brightness also depends on how efficient the bulb is. An efficient 20W bulb can be as bright as an inefficient 100W bulb, because it converts more electrical energy to light, and less to heat.

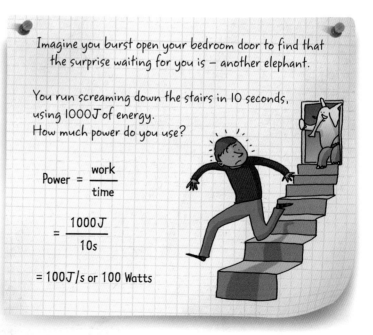

Imagine you burst open your bedroom door to find that the surprise waiting for you is – another elephant.

You run screaming down the stairs in 10 seconds, using 1000J of energy.
How much power do you use?

$$\text{Power} = \frac{\text{work}}{\text{time}}$$

$$= \frac{1000 \text{J}}{10 \text{s}}$$

$$= 100 \text{J/s or } 100 \text{ Watts}$$

The heat is on

Substances can exist in three different states: solid, liquid or gas. What state a substance is in depends on its **heat**, or 'thermal energy'.

Adding heat converts solids to liquids, and liquids to gases. That's why ice melts in warm drinks, and why steam rises from a boiling kettle. Removing heat, or cooling, reverses the process.

So how does heat melt ice?

Remember that all substances are made of atoms or molecules. Even in a solid, such as ice, all these molecules are vibrating slightly. If you warm the ice, the heat energy makes them vibrate more, and they move apart, so the ice becomes liquid water.

If you continue to heat the water, the molecules gain even more energy. This makes them move even faster and move further apart. Eventually, some of them break away, or **evaporate**, forming steam.

But if the steam hits a cool surface, like a window, it gives some of its heat energy to the window. This makes it **condense**, or become liquid again, forming water droplets.

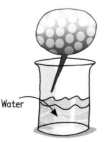

Ice

In ice, water molecules are arranged in a regular formation, touching each other.

Water

In water, the molecules spread out a bit, and are free to move past each other.

Steam

In steam, water molecules are free to whizz around and occasionally bump into each other.

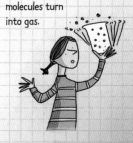

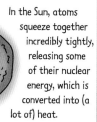
What's the difference between heat and temperature?

Temperature tells you how *hot* something is. It can be measured on three different scales – degrees Celsius (°C), degrees Fahrenheit (°F) and Kelvin (K). When something gains heat energy, its temperature rises. When it loses heat energy, its temperature falls.

Heat refers to *thermal energy*, which can be measured in joules. A warm bath is at a lower *temperature* than a steaming hot mug of tea. But because the bath is much bigger, it has more *heat energy* than the tea.

What happens to things when they're heated?

When a substance is heated, but not enough to change state, it will **expand**. This means it'll get a bit bigger and less dense. And when it's cooled, it'll **contract**, or get smaller and denser. Gases expand the most, followed by liquids. Solids expand the least.

You can see this effect for yourself. Find a jar with a really tight lid. Hold the lid under some hot water for a few moments. Then try twisting it, and it should come right off.

How does heat loosen the lid?

The jar lid loosens because of heat expansion. The heat energy passes from the hot water to the metal lid. This makes the lid expand, so it fits more loosely on the jar.

Heat expansion is what makes **thermometers** work. They contain liquids that expand or contract as they get hotter or colder. If you put a thermometer into something warm, the liquid inside it will get warm, too, and expand.

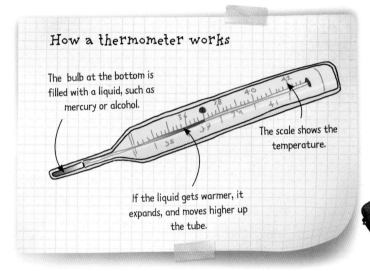

How a thermometer works

The bulb at the bottom is filled with a liquid, such as mercury or alcohol.

The scale shows the temperature.

If the liquid gets warmer, it expands, and moves higher up the tube.

Hot to trot

Heat loves to travel. It always moves from a hotter region to a cooler one – that's why an ice cream melts when you lick it. Heat energy moves from your tongue to the ice cream, so your tongue gets cooler and the ice cream gets warmer.

Heat energy moves around in three main ways. They're called **conduction**, **convection** and **radiation**. Turn the page to find out more.

Fantastic physicists

In 1724, Daniel Fahrenheit created a temperature scale based on a 'frigorific' mixture. This mixture, which combines different amounts of ice, water and ammonia salt, *always* settles at the same temperature: 0°F.

In 1742, Anders Celsius developed another scale, based on water's freezing point (0°C) and boiling point (100°C).

In 1848, William Thomson (who became Lord Kelvin) suggested a new scale, based on **absolute zero** – the temperature something would be if it had no heat energy at all. This is the scale physicists use today.

In reality, absolute zero, or 0 Kelvin, is impossible to reach. But Thomson worked out it would be equal to -273°C or -460°F.

Why do teaspoons get hot?

If you leave a cold spoon in a hot cup of tea, the spoon will get hot. This is because of conduction. **Conduction** is how heat moves through an object, or between objects that are touching. Things which are good at conducting heat, such as metal teaspoons, are called **conductors**.

Hot molecules inside the tea pass on their heat to cooler molecules on the edge of the spoon. Inside the spoon, the newly-hot molecules vibrate more than normal – making them hotter. In turn, these molecules pass on their vibrations (and heat) to any molecules they're touching, until the whole spoon is hot.

Cooking with conduction

Conduction is useful when you're cooking. You put a metal pan full of water on a hob. When you turn on the hob, heat hits the pan. The pan conducts the heat to the water – which boils and cooks your food.

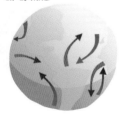

How do radiators heat up rooms?

Hot water inside a radiator heats the radiator by conduction. The radiator makes the air around it warm by radiation. But it's convection that makes the warm air near the radiator spread around in a room.

Convection is how heat is transferred in a liquid or a gas. The molecules in warm air move further apart, making the air less dense. Because it's less dense, the warm air rises, while the cool air around it sinks. When this cool air warms up, it rises too, and more cool air takes its place. This creates a cycle called a **convection current**.

Convection on a global scale

The wind is an example of a convection current on a large scale. Hot places warm the air close to them. The warm air rises, and is replaced with cool air. We feel this movement of air as wind.

Convection happens in the world's oceans, too. Warm water moves to colder areas, and cold water moves to warmer ones, creating ocean currents (shown above).

Warm air rises

Cool air replaces it

How does the Sun send out heat?

All particles emit *some* heat by **radiation**, though often it's too small too notice. But very hot things such as bonfires, or incredibly hot things such as the Sun, radiate a lot of heat.

Radiated heat moves in waves emitted by the object. These waves can even travel through empty space. The energy caried in these waves is absorbed by the things they hit, making them hot.

Absorbing heat

Heat affects some objects more than others. Dark coloured or dull things absorb more heat than light coloured or shiny things. That's why tennis players often wear white – it helps them stay cool. And solar panels which harness heat and light from the Sun are black, so they absorb as much as possible.

How do sweaters keep you warm?

Things which are bad at conducting heat, such as wood, wool or plastics, are called **insulators**. Instead of losing heat energy, they trap it.

Woollen sweaters or plastic fleeces keep you warm on cold days. Buildings are insulated too, to reduce the amount of energy needed to keep them at a comfortable temperature.

Evaporation

Heat can also be transferred by **evaporation** – when a liquid changes state and becomes a gas. The evaporating molecules have lots of heat energy. When they turn into gas, they take that energy with them, so what's left behind has less heat energy and becomes cooler.

Your body uses evaporation to cool you down. When you get hot, you sweat. The sweat evaporates and takes some heat energy with it.

See for yourself – heat absorption

Take two aluminium drink cans, and paint one black and one white.

When they're dry, put them in the Sun. Leave them for about half an hour.

Touch the cans. Which feels the warmest? The black can will probably feel hotter, because dark objects absorb more heat.

What's a wave?

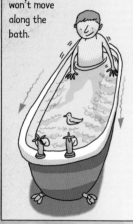

All **waves** transfer energy from place to place. If you drop a stone in a pond, you'll see waves of kinetic energy travelling outwards in ripples.

The Sun radiates waves of energy through empty space. But many other types of energy, such as sound and kinetic energy, need a substance, or **medium**, for their waves to travel through. They transfer energy by making the medium move up and down, or from side to side. This is called **oscillation**. But, although the *waves* travel, the *medium* doesn't. It oscillates and returns to its original position.

It's a bit like being part of a Mexican wave in a sports stadium. Imagine the people sitting on the opposite side of the stadium to you stand up, wave their arms about, and sit down again. Then the people to their left do the same. Soon it's your turn. Before you know it, you've stood up and sat down, and the *wave* has moved on – but *you* are exactly where you were before.

During a storm, huge waves of kinetic energy stir up the ocean, making it oscillate.

Waves to watch out for

Electromagnetic waves, and the waves you see on an ocean, are known as **transverse waves**. They wobble up and down in a shape like this:

Soundwaves are called **longitudinal waves**. They make the medium they're moving through move back and forth, squashing together and spreading apart, like this:

Peaks and troughs

This diagram shows the different parts of a transverse wave:

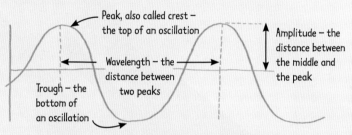

Peak, also called crest – the top of an oscillation

Amplitude – the distance between the middle and the peak

Wavelength – the distance between two peaks

Trough – the bottom of an oscillation

Wavelength (λ, or lambda) measures the distance between two peaks on the wave, and **amplitude** measures how high each peak is (both using metres). **Frequency (f)** tells you how many oscillations pass a point in one second. It's measured in **hertz (Hz)**.

   Wave speed (c), measured in m/s, tells you how fast a wave is moving. You can work out wave speed with this equation:

Wave speed (c) = frequency (f) x wavelength (λ)

For example, the speed of a soundwave in air is about 340m/s.

See for yourself: making waves

You can make transverse and longitudinal waves yourself, using a toy spring.

To make a transverse wave, hold one end of the spring in your left hand, and the other in your right hand. Move one of your hands up and down. The spring should make a transverse wave.

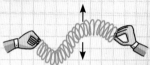

To make a longitudinal wave, push one end of the spring towards the other, then pull it back. Pulses will move from one end to the other.

If you stick a piece of tape on one of the coils and watch it as you make the waves, you'll see that it doesn't travel with the wave. It oscillates and returns to its original position.

Wave triangle

You can work out wave speed, frequency and wavelength using this magic triangle:

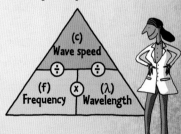

The electromagnetic spectrum

The light you can see is part of a large range, or 'spectrum', of energy waves called the **electromagnetic spectrum**. Electromagnetic energy radiates like heat – it doesn't need a medium to travel through. Each wave in the spectrum has its own wavelength and frequency, and they all have different characteristics.

The fastest thing in the Universe

As far as scientists know, the waves in the electromagnetic spectrum are the fastest things that exist. They all travel at the same speed, known as the **speed of light,** or 'c' for short. This is about 300,000,000 m/s. Electromagnetic waves can travel about 7 times round the Earth in a single second.

The Earth is 150 million km (93 million miles) from the Sun. So it takes about 8 minutes for the Sun's light to reach us. If the Sun suddenly disappeared, it would take us 8 minutes to notice.

X-rays

X-rays were discovered by a German physicist called Röntgen in 1895. He named them "X" because he didn't know much about them.

X-rays pass through flesh but are absorbed by dense things such as bones or metal. So doctors use X-ray images to see if you've broken your arm, or swallowed something strange.

This diagram shows the main types of energy wave found across the electromagnetic spectrum.

Shortest wavelength, highest frequency

Time travel physics

It's impossible to travel at the speed of light. But one day people might be able to go *almost* as fast. Physicists predict that at this immense speed, *time would slow down*.

Imagine you could travel off into space at near-light speed for five years. When you got back home, all your friends would be five years older. You'd be five years older, too, but because time was moving so slowly for you, you'd look and feel the same age as the day you left.

Gamma rays

Gamma rays can travel through almost anything, even lead. If they pass through your body they can cause cancer, which can be deadly. Gamma rays are given off by substances that send out energy from the nuclei of their atoms. These are known as **radioactive** substances.

DANGER

This symbol means something is radioactive.

Ultraviolet waves

Ultraviolet waves come from the Sun and are the reason you get a suntan. But too many of them can damage your skin.

Really long, really short

The longest wavelengths are as big as the Universe. The shortest are as small as the tiniest particles inside atoms.

Visible light

This is the light our eyes can see. It's really made up of many different colours, all with different wavelengths.

Microwaves

Microwaves don't just heat food up quickly. They're also used in radar, to locate distant objects. Radar transmitters fire out microwaves, which bounce back when they hit something. Radar operators can work out how far away that thing is from the amount of time it takes the waves to return.

Fantastic physicist: Albert Einstein 1879-1955

Albert Einstein was the first person to work out the strange things that happen at the speed of light. Because it's impossible to travel that fast, he conducted 'thought experiments' and imagined it instead.

Einstein loved maths and wanted to be a teacher when he left school. But he couldn't find a teaching job, so he became a clerk in a patents office, and studied physics in his spare time.

Longest wavelength, lowest frequency

Infra-red radiation

Infra-red is a kind of heat – it's radiation produced by hot objects. If you were hiding in the dark, someone could use an infra-red detector to find you. That's because your body is warmer than your surroundings, so you'd give off more infra-red radiation.

Radiowaves

All sorts of messages are sent using radiowaves. They're used to broadcast radio programmes, and to transmit mobile phone and wireless internet signals.

Energy equals...

In 1905, Einstein published four theories which completely changed what scientists believe about light, space and time.

One of his theories included the equation: $E = mc^2$. In words, this says 'the amount of energy in an object (E) equals its mass (m) times the speed of light squared (c^2)'.

This means that even something with a tiny mass – such as an atom – contains loads of energy. This idea helped other scientists to invent the atomic bomb.

A photo of a dog taken with an infra-red camera

Let there be light!

If you're reading this book, there must be a light source near you – whether it's the Sun or an electric light or even a candle.

Without light you wouldn't be able to see anything at all. The reason you see things is because light waves shine out from a light source, bounce off different objects, and then go into your eyes.

Seeing the light

When some objects get really hot – above about 600°C – they glow.

This is how the Sun, fires and some kinds of light bulbs work. Physicists call them 'luminous bodies' because they send out light that we can see.

See-through science

You can't see someone through a brick wall, because bricks are **opaque**. That means light can't travel through them.

Windows, on the other hand, are see-through or **transparent** – meaning light can travel through them.

There are some objects, such as frosted glass, which are semi-see-through or **translucent**. Some light can travel through them, but the path is disrupted so you don't get a clear image of what's on the other side.

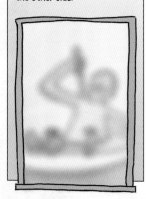

Why can't we see around corners?

Well, you *can* see around corners – but only if you use a mirror (and you can find out more about *that* over the page). Light waves travel in a straight line. You can see this if you stand in a dark room and shine a torch on the wall. Light waves can't turn corners or bend of their own accord – they have to hit something first.

Where do shadows come from?

Opaque objects (things you can't see through) cast shadows because light can't pass through them. Instead, they absorb or reflect light, leaving a black area behind them. The size and shape of the shadows depend on where the light is coming from.

When a light source, such as the Sun, is directly overhead, you only cast a tiny shadow, like this:

But when the Sun is low in the sky, your shadow looks really long and thin, like this:

What makes a rainbow?

Light is actually a mix of different colours. When you see a rainbow, you're seeing all the different colours, separated by droplets of water in the air.

Each colour of light has a slightly different wavelength, so they all behave a bit differently. When each colour hits a transparent object, such as a drop of rain, it moves through it at a slightly different speed. This makes the colours separate and spread out.

Newton's solar spectrum

Isaac Newton was the first person to show that white light is made up of different colours.

One sunny day, he covered up the windows in his room, all except for one tiny hole which let a beam of sunlight through. He put a prism in front of it, and it bent the light into a pattern of colours on his wall. He called this the **solar spectrum**.

The photograph on the right shows light being split into its different colours using a triangular chunk of glass called a prism.

There are seven colours, which always split up in the order of their wavelengths. Red (the longest) splits at the widest angle, followed by orange, yellow, green, blue, indigo and lastly, violet.

Lights hits a prism and is split into rays of different colours

Seeing colours

Just as objects absorb different amounts of heat, they also absorb different amounts — and colours — of light.

Shiny objects look bright and shiny because they bounce back lots of light. White objects are often bright because don't absorb *any* light. Instead, it all bounces off them and into your eyes. Black objects absorb *all* colours. Nothing bounces off, which is why they look black.

Other objects absorb all the colours *except* for the colour they appear to be. For example, grass absorbs most colours, but bounces green light back. That's why grass looks green. People who are colour-blind aren't able to see certain colours because their eyes can't detect that wavelength.

Colour mixing

Although there are seven colours of light in the rainbow, it's possible to use just three of them to make all the rest.

These three colours — red, blue and green — are known as the primary colours of light.

If you shine rays of red, blue and green light all in the same place, they'll produce white light.

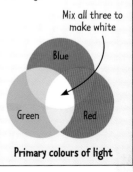

Mix all three to make white

Blue

Green   Red

Primary colours of light

55

Reflecting light

All surfaces reflect some light – if they didn't, we wouldn't be able to see them. But some surfaces are better at reflecting light than others. Smooth, shiny, light-coloured things reflect more light than dull, uneven, dark things. This is why you can see your face reflected in a flat, shiny mirror and not in a dark, bumpy tree.

The rule of reflection

If you throw a ball straight at a wall, it will bounce straight back at you. And if you throw it from one side, at an angle, it will bounce back at the same angle on the opposite side. This is called the **rule of reflection**, and it works for light, too.

Ball thrown straight at a wall

Ball thrown at an angle

You can try it yourself by shining a torch at a mirror. If you shine it straight at the mirror the light will bounce straight back at you. That's because you're shining it along the **normal** – an imaginary line at right angles to the surface of the mirror.

More about mirrors

Everything you see in a mirror is the wrong way around. That's why the writing on a book or newspaper always appears back to front in a mirror.

When you stand close to the mirror, and then walk away from it, your reflection moves exactly the same distance away in the mirror.

Meow, that's bright

'Catseyes' are road markings which light up when headlights shine on them. They're called catseyes because they appear to shine in the dark in the same way as real cats' eyes.

Artificial catseyes contain balls of glass with a reflective coating inside. When light hits them, it bounces back out again. The reflected light shows drivers where they are on the road.

But if you shine the torch at an angle, the light will bounce off the mirror at an equal and opposite angle on the other side of the normal.

The angle at which the light hits the mirror is called the **angle of incidence**. The angle the light makes when it bounces back is called the **angle of reflection**.

The rule of reflection

This is how your physics teacher might teach you the rule of reflection:

The angle of incidence = the angle of reflection

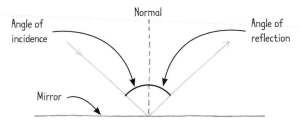

Normal

Angle of incidence

Angle of reflection

Mirror

Scattering light

The rule of reflection only works for a completely flat, smooth mirror, known as a plane mirror. Uneven surfaces reflect light in all different directions. Physicists call this **scattering**. Curved or bumpy surfaces form wonky reflections, and some scatter light so much that you can't see any reflection at all.

If you look at yourself in a curved mirror, your reflection will look quite strange.

Why is the sky blue?

As light passes through the atmosphere, the colours with longer wavelengths (red and orange) pass straight through. Colours with shorter wavelengths (blue and violet) are scattered by the air. This makes the sky overhead look blue.

If you look into the distance, the sky will be a paler blue. That's because more distant light must pass through more air to reach you. Some of the blue light gets scattered away in other directions, so less of it reaches your eyes.

Total internal reflection

Nothing there... you must be hungry.

Sometimes light can be trapped inside a substance because it reflects again and again and again. This is called **total internal reflection (t.i.r.)**.

Usually, some light waves are absorbed by their surroundings. But in t.i.r. light is **totally** reflected (as the name suggests) — so none is absorbed as the light travels. This can be very useful.

Fibre optic cables use t.i.r. to carry light signals for telephones, the internet and televisions. Because no light is lost, they can transmit very clear, strong signals a really long way. It works like this:

Flexible fibre optics

Fibre optic cables are very flexible. The fibres are thin and bendy, so they're often used in medical procedures.

When someone gets a really nasty tummy ache, a doctor might push a fibre optic cable with a tiny camera on it down their mouth, to see what's going on inside their stomach.

A computer modem converts electricity into light signals.

These travel along a fibre-optic cable by total internal reflection.

The signals arrive at another computer which converts them back into electricity.

Why does a straw look bent when it's in a glass of water?

Light bends when it enters water, making this straw look bent.

Sometimes, a straw in a glass of water looks bent or broken. But it's the light, not the straw, that's bent.

Light travels at different speeds in different mediums. It slows down as it enters water — just as you'd slow down if you ran into a pond — and it speeds up again when it re-enters the air. As it slows down or speeds up, it bends. This is known as **refraction**.

How can refraction help you see?

Glasses, telescopes, microscopes and cameras all contain **lenses** – specially cut pieces of plastic or glass that curve inwards (concave) or outwards (convex).

Lenses **focus** light waves by refracting the light entering the lens. Combinations of lenses in magnifying glasses and telescopes help to form a clear image of an object that's too tiny or far away to see with the naked eye. There are two main types of lens:

Why do some people need glasses?

Lenses aren't just manmade objects. They also occur in nature – in your eyes, for example.

The lenses in your eyes are very sophisticated. They can change shape to help your eyes focus on objects that are either nearby or far away.

Some people's lenses don't change shape so easily, so they wear glasses or contacts – an extra set of lenses in front of their eyes.

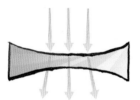

A **concave** lens refracts
light outwards

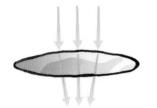

A **convex** lens refracts
light inwards

Make your own magnifying glass

If you follow the instructions, you can make a very simple sort of magnifying glass using an empty plastic bottle, some water, and a pair of scissors.

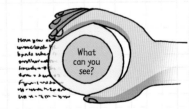

What can you see?

I. Cut a disc out of the bottle, from just below the neck – where the bottle is curved.

2. Pour a little water into the disc.

3. Hold it above a newspaper and move it around.

What happens?

You should find that the writing looks larger when you look at it through the water-filled disc. The water and the plastic are refracting the light and acting as a lens.

Hearing things

The reason you hear things is because of sound energy. Sounds are produced when things – such as the strings on a violin – vibrate.

The molecules in the strings vibrate and bump into any air molecules next to them, making them vibrate, too. The vibrations are passed through the air in a continuous wave. Eventually the vibrations reach your eardrums, making *them* vibrate – and you hear the noise.

Why are some sounds high-pitched and others low-pitched?

When something vibrates fast, the waves it sends out move fast, too. The waves produced when something vibrates very fast are known as **high frequency** sound waves. When something vibrates more slowly it produces **low frequency** sound waves.

High frequency waves make high-pitched, squeaky noises – like a shrill scream, or a car alarm. Low frequency waves make low-pitched, rumbly noises – like a big dog growling or a truck's engine chugging.

Wave frequency is measured in **hertz (Hz)**, so the pitch of a sound is measured in hertz, too. Humans can't hear all frequencies – our ears only pick up sounds between 20,000Hz-20Hz. Some animals, such as dogs and bats, can hear much higher frequency sounds than we can.

Sound waves with frequencies higher than 20,000Hz are known as **ultrasound**, and those below 20Hz are known as **infrasound**.

See for yourself: sound waves

Sound waves can be pretty powerful: if you put your hand in front of a speaker you can feel it making the air move.

If you want to *see* what sound waves can do, put some little bits of paper on top of a speaker and turn the volume up. The vibrations from the sound waves will make the tissue paper jump.

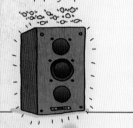

How can you tell how far away a storm is?

Thunder is actually the sound lightning makes when it zig-zags through the sky. Sound travels more slowly than light, so you always hear thunder *after* you've seen lightning.

If you want to know how far you are from a lightning strike, count the seconds between the time you see it and the time you hear thunder. Divide the number of seconds by 3 to see how many kilometres away you are, or by 5 to get the number of miles.

What a quiet, well-behaved class you are!

Studying sound

Sound waves are invisible, but physicists can use a machine called an **oscilloscope** to 'see' them. A microphone picks up vibrations and the oscilloscope changes them into wave patterns on a screen. These patterns show the sound's frequency and **amplitude** (how loud it is).

If you ever become a famous singer, you'll see your producer fiddling around with a screen like this in the recording studio, trying to get your voice to sound even better than it already is. They can adjust the amplitude, to make your voice louder or quieter, and alter the frequency, which changes the pitch — so you always sound in tune.

Ageing ears

As you get older, the range of noise frequencies you can hear gradually reduces. Most children can hear higher frequencies than their parents and teachers, for example.

Some mobile phone ring tones are deliberately high-pitched, so that children can hear them when they ring, but adults can't.

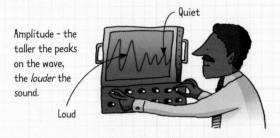

Quiet

Amplitude - the taller the peaks on the wave, the *louder* the sound.

Loud

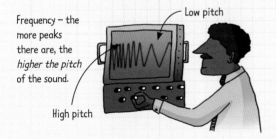

Low pitch

Frequency – the more peaks there are, the *higher the pitch* of the sound.

High pitch

Higher and lower

Here are some of the frequencies of different sounds:

100,000 – 14,000Hz – bat squeaks

5,000 – 4,000Hz – cricket song

4,500 – 100Hz – piano notes

2,048Hz – highest note a singer can reach

1,000 – 450Hz – human speaking voice

30 – 17Hz – blue whale calls

5–1Hz – tornado

Keep it down!

Sound amplitude is measured in **decibels (dB)**. A quiet whisper is about 30dB. Talking normally is about 60dB. Sounds above about 100dB can damage your hearing and even make you deaf.

How do echoes happen?

Echoes are reflected sound waves. If you shout in a big, empty room, the sound you make travels to the wall and then bounces – or echoes – back to you. The further the sound travels, the quieter it gets.

Where's the best place to hear echoes?

Sound vibrations reflect best from hard, flat, solid surfaces. But the surface has to be quite far away for you to hear a distinct echo. If it's too close, you just hear a continuous noise.

You can hear top quality echoes in big places, such as an empty church or an underground cave.

Are echoes useful?

They're very useful, especially to bats. Bats hunt at night, when their prey can't see them. But they can't see their prey, either. Instead, they send out high-pitched squeaks and wait for the sound waves to bounce back to them. By listening to the way the waves return, they can build up a picture of what's around them, and work out if food is nearby.

The bat sends out high-pitched sounds.

The sound waves hit a moth (tasty food for a bat) and bounce back.

Seeing a baby before it's born

Doctors use ultrasound – high frequency sounds that humans can't hear – to look at babies while they're still inside their mothers. Soundwaves are beamed inside the mother, and they bounce off the baby.

Engineers have built machines that copy this bat method of seeing in the dark. They call the method **SONAR** – Sound Navigation and Ranging.

Battleship crews use SONAR to look for enemy submarines hidden underwater. The ship sends out a pinging sound, and waits for microphones to pick up the echoes. Most echoes bounce back off the sea bed, but shorter echoes might reveal a hidden submarine.

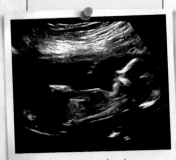

An ultrasound picture of a baby in the womb

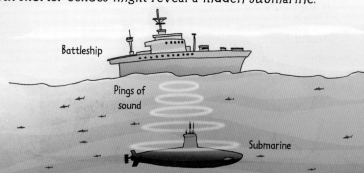

Battleship

Pings of sound

Submarine

Sound vs. light: the showdown

Light travels faster than sound. But sound can be powerful enough to make your teeth rattle, or even make you deaf.

Sound and light waves have different strengths. So if they had a 'Top Wave' contest, it's hard to say who'd win. But it might go a bit like this...

Challenge 1:
Travelling around corners

Light looks as if it has the upper hand as it speeds along towards the corner much faster than sound. But unless there's a mirror in the right place, it'll shoot right past.

Sound spreads out and even passes through things, so it has no trouble coping with the corner.

Result: Sound wins. So remember that if you're hiding from someone, you need to keep as quiet as possible even when you've found a really good hiding place.

Challenge 2:
Travelling through space

Light speeds off, as usual, and keeps going strongly until the finishing line.

Sound doesn't even get off the starting block. Sound waves need a medium to travel through, and empty space isn't a medium.

Result: Light wins. Sound travels when vibrations are passed on from particle to particle. There aren't many particles in space (there isn't much of anything in space – hence its name) which is why in space, no one can hear you scream...

Challenge 3:
Travelling through a window

Light slows down once it enters the glass. And it gets refracted, too, so the image it shows you might be a bit wonky, depending on the quality of the glass.

Sound actually speeds up in glass. Sound waves travel more quickly in solids (and even in liquids) than in gases like air. That's because the particles in solids and liquids are closer together, so they pass on vibrations more quickly. But the sound is muffled by the glass, so it's quieter on the other side.

Result: it's a tie! Both sound and light get through the window, but they're both altered by it.

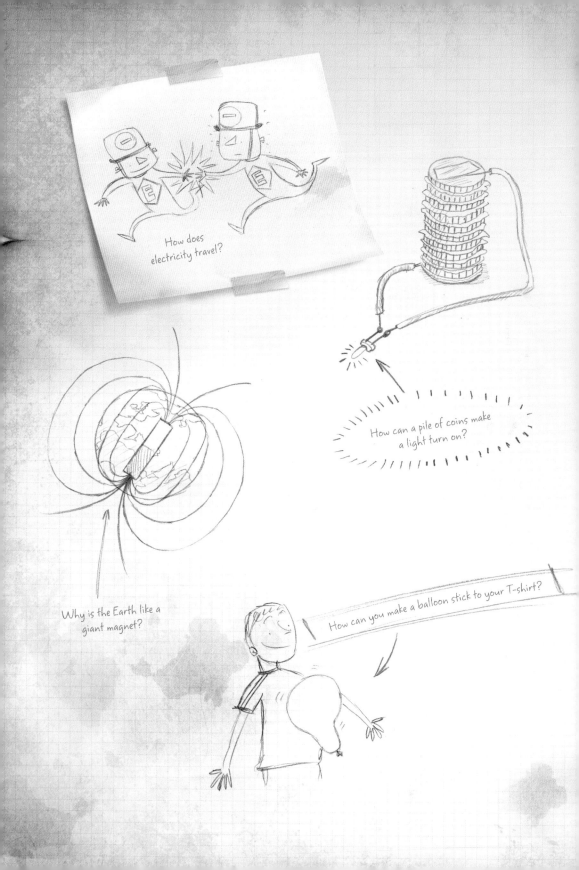

How does electricity travel?

How can a pile of coins make a light turn on?

Why is the Earth like a giant magnet?

How can you make a balloon stick to your T-shirt?

Part 4:
It's electrifying

Electricity is a kind of energy that comes in two different forms. *Static electricity* is the kind that makes your hair cling to your clothes when you pull them over your head. It's also what makes lightning flash through the sky. *Current electricity* is what flows through wires. This is the kind that's used to power televisions, computers, lights and heaters, as well as many, many other things people rely on every day.

Both kinds of electricity are related, but where do they come from? Read on to find out.

Where does electricity come from?

Lightning rods

Lightning striking the Eiffel Tower in Paris

Lightning often strikes tall buildings, which can set them on fire. Tall buildings, including the Eiffel Tower, are protected by lightning rods – strips of metal that let the lightning flow through them safely to the ground. This means the electricity can spread out into the Earth without causing any damage.

Electricity is all to do with electrons – the negatively charged particles found in atoms. Overall, an atom has no charge, because its electrons are balanced out by positively charged protons. But *if any electrons are added or taken away*, the atom ends up with either a positive or negative **electric charge**.

How can that happen?

Believe it or not, it can happen to some objects very easily. If you rub a plastic balloon against a cotton T-shirt, some of the electrons will come off the T-shirt and stick to the balloon. This gives the balloon a slight negative charge, and the T-shirt a slight positive charge. Opposite charges attract, so you should find that the balloon sticks to the T-shirt.

Plastic and wool are both types of **insulators** – substances that build up an electric charge, rather than passing it on (similar to insulators which store up heat). This build-up of charge creates the kind of electrical energy known as **static electricity**.

Static electricity can be extremely powerful. For example, during stormy weather, water droplets in clouds rub together. This can build up a huge negative charge at the bottom of the cloud. The cloud will get rid of, or **discharge**, this build-up of charge by sending a bolt of lightning through the sky to a point of opposite charge, such as the top of another cloud, or the ground below.

66

Repelling and attracting

Two objects with opposite charges will attract each other. But if they've got the same charge, they'll push each other away, or **repel** each other.

You can test this using two empty plastic bottles. Rub one against your T-shirt, so it gets a negative charge, then rest it on a table, on its side. Now charge up the other bottle, and bring it close to the first bottle. They should repel each other, making the first bottle roll away.

Here's another experiment to show how static electricity attracts things.

Give a balloon a negative charge by rubbing it on your T-shirt, then hold it against a wall, and move your hand away. The balloon should stick to the wall, even though walls don't usually have a charge.

The balloon's negative charge repels the electrons on the very edge of the wall, leaving the wall with a slight positive charge. So the balloon and wall attract each other.

What about the electricity people use at home?

The electricity that flows through the wires in your home isn't static. It's called **current electricity** and, instead of building up in a substance, it flows through it. But how does this happen? Turn the page to find out.

To conduct, or not to conduct?

Some substances, such as silicon, can be insulators when they're cold, and conductors when they're hot. These substances are called **semiconductors**.

Computer chips are made from semiconductors. They're essential components to make all sorts of machines work, from mobile phones to microwaves to MP3 players.

Two kinds of electricity

Static electricity is a build-up of charged particles in a substance. It's the kind of electricity that gives you a shock if you shuffle over the carpet in your trainers and then touch a metal door handle – you're feeling the electricity discharge.

Current electricity is the movement of electrical charge through a substance, and between substances. It's what you get from an electric socket.

How can electricity flow?

Electricity can flow through a substance called a **conductor**. Metals such as copper are good conductors, which is why electricians use them to make wires. In a metal, there are loosely held electrons which flow around the molecules in a sort of cloud. These electrons can pass on electrical charge very easily.

The flow of electric charge through a conductor is called an **electric current**.

What creates an electric current?

Current doesn't just flow through a wire of its own accord — it needs a power source such as a **battery**.

Batteries build up a large amount of electrons — and so, a large amount of negative charge — at one end, called the **negative terminal**. The other end (the **positive terminal**) has far fewer electrons.

If you connect a wire to one end of the battery — nothing happens. But if you then connect the other end of the wire to the *other* end of the battery, the electrons at the negative terminal will pass their charge all the way along the wire to the positive terminal. In other words, a current will flow through it.

Racing electrons

Electricity flows through wires, but individual electrons don't race all the way around themselves.

Instead each one bumps into the one next to it, and so on, passing on energy a bit like a relay race, or a tumbling row of dominoes.

Fantastic physicists: Galvani and Volta 16th–17th century

Luigi Galvani noticed that a dead frog's leg twitched when it was touched by a conductor with an electric charge in it, but he couldn't work out why.

Rival scientist Alessandro Volta suggested that *charge* was flowing through it. He went on to create the first useable battery. The amount of charge a battery holds is known as 'voltage' in his honour.

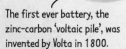

The first ever battery, the zinc-carbon 'voltaic pile', was invented by Volta in 1800.

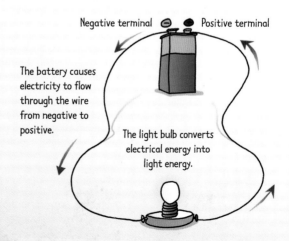

Negative terminal ⊖ ● Positive terminal

The battery causes electricity to flow through the wire from negative to positive.

The light bulb converts electrical energy into light energy.

How do batteries work?

A battery is a store of chemical energy that can be converted into electrical energy. The batteries most people use at home contain a paste called an **electrolyte**, and two metal terminals.

Chemical reactions in the electrolyte force electrons to build up at the negative terminal, while a positive charge builds up at the postive terminal. The difference in charge between the terminals is called **voltage**.

The voltage of a battery determines how *powerful* it is – to be specific, how much current it will drive through a conductor. Voltage is measured in **volts (V)**, often written on the side of the battery, and it can be measured using a device called a **voltmeter**.

AC/DC

There are two kinds of electric current – **direct current (DC)** and **alternating current (AC)**.

Direct current is the kind you get from batteries. It flows continuously in one direction.

Alternating current is what supplies the electricity in your house. It's provided by fast-spinning generators in power stations.

AC is more efficient because a current will always flow as long as the generator keeps spinning. But a battery will eventually run out, and need recharging.

Make your own battery

You'll need:

half a cup of salt; a cup of vinegar; 11 copper coins;
10 circles of coffee filter paper, and 10 circles of aluminium foil, each the same size as the coins

Mix the salt and vinegar together – this will be your electrolyte.

Leave the filter paper to soak in the electrolyte for a few minutes.

You build the battery in layers. Each layer has a coin at the bottom, then a circle of foil, then a circle of filter paper. Keep piling up layers **in the same order** until you end up with just a coin on top. Don't let the foil touch more than one coin, or another piece of foil.

Leave the finished battery to 'charge' for a few minutes.

To test your battery, you'll need:

Two copper wires and a light-emitting diode (LED) (you can buy these things from a DIY shop)

Connect one end of each wire to the LED by twisting it around the LED's terminals. Now tape one end of one wire underneath the battery. Tape the end of the other wire on top of the battery. When both ends are touching a coin, the LED should light up.

The current wars

In 1882, Thomas Edison was the first person to supply people with electricity. He used DC.

But then his great rival, Nikola Tesla, told the US government that AC was more efficient. Edison worried he'd lose money, and tried to persuade people AC was dangerous by using it to electrocute animals.

But in the end, AC became more popular, because Tesla was right. AC *is* more efficient than DC – and it's cheaper to supply, too.

Electricity at home

The current electricity supplied to our homes is called **mains electricity**, and it's supplied at very high voltages. So, for safety, all electric plugs contain fuses, which melt and break the circuit if too much current flows through them.

Most electric appliances also contain something called an **earth wire**. If too much voltage builds up, the earth wire carries the current into the ground, so it doesn't give anyone an electric shock.

Current triangle

Here's a magic triangle to show how to work out current, charge and time:

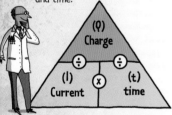

Resistance in wires

The *longer* a wire is, the more resistance it has, because the current has to flow through more of it.

The *thicker* a wire is, the less resistance it has, because there's more room in it for the current to flow.

Going around in circuits

An electric current flowing through a wire is a very basic example of a **circuit**. Most circuits include other parts, called **components**, which make use of the current that flows through them. For example, a component called a **motor** inside an electric toothbrush converts electric current into kinetic energy.

To work, a component needs a certain amount of current. If the current isn't strong enough, there isn't enough power for the component to turn on.

Calculating current

Current (I) is a measure of how much **charge (Q)** is flowing through a circuit at a particular moment. Charge is measured in **coulombs**, so current is measured in coulombs per second — more commonly known as **amperes**, or **amps** for short. You can measure current with a component called an **ammeter**, or you can work it out with this formula:

$$\text{current (amps)} = \frac{\text{charge (coulombs)}}{\text{time (seconds)}} \quad \text{or:} \quad I = \frac{Q}{t}$$

Resisting current

Just as friction slows down moving objects, **resistance** reduces the flow of current. **Resistance (R)** is measured in **ohms**. Insulators, such as plastics, have a high resistance, while conductors, such as metals, have a low resistance.

You can calculate resistance using this formula:

$$\text{resistance (ohms)} = \frac{\text{voltage (volts)}}{\text{current (amps)}} \quad \text{or:} \quad R = \frac{V}{I}$$

Two types of circuit

You can arrange components in two different kinds of circuit: **in series** or **in parallel**. For example, a string of fairy lights can be wired up either way. Each has different effects on the lights.

In series

Fairy lights connected in a series circuit use just one long wire, with each bulb lined up in a row, one after the other. Current passes through each one in turn, and each bulb converts the electricity to light.

Series circuits are cheap to make, but they cause two problems. Firstly, if one bulb blows, it breaks the circuit, so *none* of the bulbs light up.

Secondly, a series circuit with lots of bulbs has a high resistance. This reduces the voltage, so each bulb only has a dim glow.

In parallel

In a parallel circuit, each bulb is placed on its own separate section of wire. This needs more wire, but it reduces problems. The current has more than one path to travel down, so the same amount of current flows to each bulb.

This means they all glow with the same brightness. And if one bulb blows, it won't break the whole circuit.

Wire safety

Electrical wires are made of metal and covered with plastic insulators, to stop the electrical charge getting out — and giving you a shock.

Home safety

Keep electrical appliances away from water. Water is a good conductor of electricity, so if any water leaks into the device it'll conduct the current. This will stop the device working, and could give you a fatal shock if you're touching the water as well.

Make sure all wires are properly insulated. If you can see bits of metal through the plastic coating, beware — an exposed wire that's connected to the mains could give you a deadly shock or start a fire.

Devices that convert electricity into heat, such as kettles and toasters, need a lot of current. If you plug two or more of these devices into the same socket, and switch them on at the same time, it may make the socket overheat and catch fire.

More about circuits

When a battery isn't a battery

Physicists don't actually call the batteries you use at home 'batteries'. In physics, they're called **cells**. A *battery* is when two or more cells are joined together.

The circuit symbol for a cell looks like this:

The symbol for a battery looks like this:

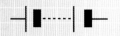

Back to front

Current is a flow of electrons from negative to positive. But in circuit diagrams, current is drawn flowing from the *positive* to the *negative* terminal. Why?

The first person to realize that current flows from one terminal of a cell to the other was French physicist André Ampère. He was working in the 18th century, before electrons were discovered. He thought that current flowed from positive to negative.

By the time his mistake was discovered, so many circuit diagrams had been drawn that physicists decided to keep drawing them in the same way.

The direction current is drawn in circuit diagrams is known as **conventional current**, but the direction current actually flows is called **real current**.

It can be easier to think about how a circuit works if you draw a diagram of it. The diagram needs to show which parts of the circuit are connected to each other. Physicists use symbols to represent components in the circuit, and draw straight lines to show the wires.

When you're drawing a circuit diagram, use a ruler to draw the lines, and make sure there are no gaps, or it'll look as if the circuit is broken.

Here's an example of a basic circuit diagram:

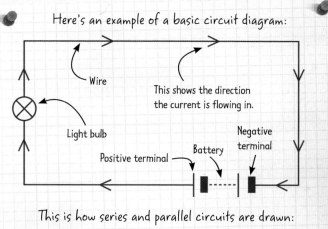

Wire

This shows the direction the current is flowing in.

Light bulb

Positive terminal — Battery

Negative terminal

This is how series and parallel circuits are drawn:

Series circuit

Cell

Light bulbs

A cell is the basic component of a battery.

Cell

Parallel circuit

Light bulb

Here are some of the symbols for different
components you might find in a circuit.

Switch — open

When a switch is open (off), the
circuit is broken, so current
can't flow.

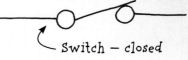

Switch — closed

When a switch is closed (on), it completes
the circuit, so current flows.

Voltmeter

A voltmeter measures the amount of
voltage in a circuit. It won't give an
accurate reasding unless it's connected
in a parallel circuit.

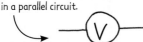

Ammeter

An ammeter measures the amount
of current in a circuit. It won't give a
proper reading unless it's connected
in a series circuit.

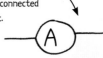

Diode

A diode is made from a
semiconductor and only conducts
electricity in one direction.

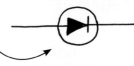

Light emitting diode (LED)

A diode that gives out light when
electricity flows through it the
right way. Uses very little energy, so
it's used in energy efficient lights.

Variable resistor

Changes the amount of resistance
in a circuit, to control the amount
of current flowing through it.

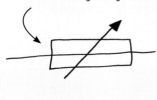

Fuse

A fuse makes sure only a safe
amount of current flows through
a circuit.

Thermistor

A type of resistor with resistance
which *decreases* as temperature
increases. Used to measure and control
temperature in heating and cooling
systems and microwave ovens.

Chip chip hooray!

Modern computer chips
are tiny – no bigger than
your fingertip – but they
contain millions of circuits.
Before chips were invented,
the circuits used to make
computers work were huge.
So it was impossible to have
really small electrical devices.

Physicists are finding ways
to make circuits smaller all
the time.

Why do magnets stick to your fridge?

Magnetic words

Ferromagnetic – a substance that is strongly magnetic, or can be magnetized easily, such as iron.

Magnetically hard – a substance which doesn't easily lose its magnetism once it's been magnetized, e.g. steel. Used to make permanent magnets.

Magnetically soft – a substance which doesn't stay magnetized for long, e.g. iron. Used to make temporary magnets.

A **magnet** is something which can exert **magnetic force**. This means it has the ability to attract certain magnetic metals, including iron, steel, cobalt and nickel. Fridges are usually made of steel, so if you put a magnet on your fridge door, it'll probably stay there.

Magnets can attract or repel other magnets, too. That's because they have two opposite ends, called **poles** – one 'north' and one 'south' (the underside of a fridge magnet is one pole, the topside is the other).

Like electrical charges, opposite poles attract, and like poles repel. If you put one fridge magnet on top of the other, they'll stick together. But if you try to push the undersides together, they'll push each other away.

What makes a magnet magnetic?

Some substances are naturally magnetic. Magnetism was discovered thousands of years ago, when people noticed that a rock called lodestone could attract iron.

But magnets can be created, too. It's easy to magnetize iron and steel, for example (turn the page to find out how to do it yourself). The molecules in these metals act as miniature 'molecular' magnets, with their own north and south poles.

Imagining magnets

Inside magnetic substances, there are 'molecular magnets', each with their own north and south poles. You can use matches to see how they're arranged in magnetized and unmagnetized substances.

Imagine tipping a pile of matches onto a table. The matches are all jumbled up, just like the molecular magnets in an unmagnetized substance.

Imagine lining up all the matches so their heads face the same way. That's how the molecular magnets in a magnet are arranged.

Usually, when a bar of iron is unmagnetized, its molecular magnets point all over the place.

But when the bar is magnetized, its molecular magnets all point in the same direction.

Magnetic patterns

There's a forcefield around every magnet, called the **magnetic field**, where the magnetic force is strongest. The force created by a magnetic field makes invisble patterns called **magnetic field lines**. These lines change when two magnets meet.

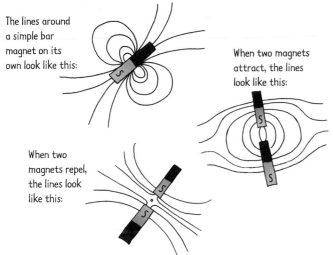

The lines around a simple bar magnet on its own look like this:

When two magnets attract, the lines look like this:

When two magnets repel, the lines look like this:

Magnetic migration

All sorts of creatures, from turtles to birds to butterflies, travel thousands of miles every year, to find cool places in summer and warmer places in winter. Often they've never made the trip before, but they almost always end up in the right place.

That's because the Earth itself is a giant magnet, and these animals can sense the Earth's magnetic field, which tells them if they're going in the right direction.

Seeing magnetic field lines

Although it's impossible to see the magnetic field itself, you can use iron filings to see the pattern of field lines it creates.

You will need:

- A bar magnet   - Iron filings   - A piece of paper

Lay the piece of paper on top of the bar magnet. Sprinkle some iron filings on top. Gently tap the piece of paper, so the iron filings jump up and then fall down on the paper again.

What happens?

The iron filings will make a pattern around the magnet, which shows the strength and direction of the magnetic force.

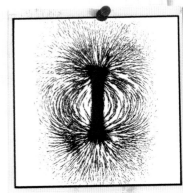

When you sprinkle iron filings over a magnet, they make a pattern like this.

How to make a magnet

You can make all the molecules in iron or steel point the same way by stroking the metal repeatedly with another magnet. Try it yourself:

You will need:

A bar magnet

Two steel needles

Destroying magnets

Magnets can be destroyed by jumbling up the molecular magnets. One way to do this is to hit a magnet with a hammer. Another is to heat it until it's red hot. But don't try either of these at home.

1. Stroke one of the needles with the bar magnet in the same direction, about 10 times.

2. Now take the needle you've stroked and touch the other needle with it.

What happens?

You should find the stroked needle attracts the other needle strongly enough to pick it up. You've made the first needle into a magnet.

See for yourself: Earth's magnetism

Use the method described above to magnetise a needle. Fill a cup with water, and place the magnetised needle on the water, in the middle of the cup.

The needle should move around and gradually come to rest. It's being attracted by the Earth's magnetic field. The needle will rest in line with the Earth's North Magnetic Pole – just like the needle on a compass.

What's the biggest magnet on Earth?

The Earth itself – it's actually a giant magnet. It has a solid core surrounded by liquid iron, which acts like a bar magnet running through the middle of the planet.

The top end of the magnetic field, or the 'magnetic North Pole', is very near to, but not quite in the same place as, the 'geographic' North Pole (the North Pole you see on a map). The other end of the magnetic field is very close to the geographic South Pole.

The needle of a compass points towards the magnetic North Pole, because it's attracted to the Earth's magnetic field – unless there's a powerful magnet nearby to distract it.

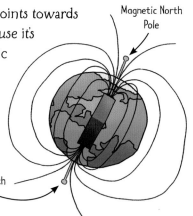

Magnetic North Pole

Magnetic South Pole

This diagram shows the pattern of the Earth's magnetic field.

Why am I reading about magnets in a chapter about electricity?

Electricity and magnetism are very closely linked. Electric current always creates a magnetic field around it. So, when a current flows through a wire, the wire temporarily becomes a magnet, even if it isn't magnetic the rest of the time. The greater the current, the stronger the magnetic field it creates. This is called **electromagnetism**.

Electromagnetism can create really strong, temporary magnets called **electromagnets**. These are made by wrapping a long coil of wire around an iron core and passing a current through it.

Magnets can cause a current to flow, too. If you spin a magnet around inside a coil of wire, voltage builds up in the wire. If the wire is connected to a circuit, current will flow around it. The stronger the field and the faster the movement, the more voltage is produced.

Inside a power station, water is boiled into steam. This steam turns a machine called a turbine, which in turn spins a magnet around inside a coil of wire, , generating an electric current that can be sent to people's homes.

See for yourself — electromagnets

You can make your own electromagnet using some insulated copper wire, a battery, an iron nail and some paperclips.

Wind the wire around the nail, keeping the coils very close together. Wind the ends of the wire around the battery terminals. Hold the nail near the paperclips and see what happens.

You should find the nail picks up the paperclips. That's because it's turned into an electromagnet. But if you disconnect the wire from the battery, it won't work. It's only a magnet when current flows through it.

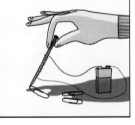

Hovering trains

Some countries, including Japan and the USA, have really fast trains called Maglev trains.

These trains have electromagnets underneath them, and they run on tracks made of electromagnets. The magnets repel each other, so the train never touches the tracks. There's no friction between the train and track, which makes Maglev trains really speedy and efficient.

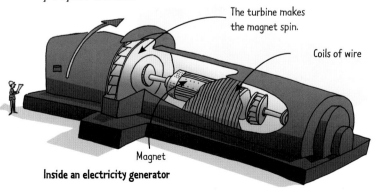

The turbine makes the magnet spin.

Coils of wire

Magnet

Inside an electricity generator

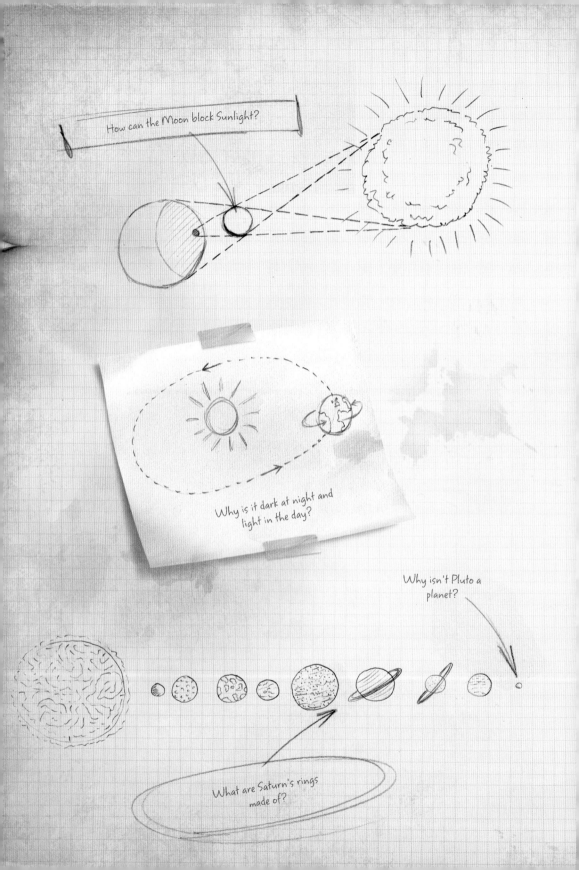

Part 5:
Lost in space

Space is vast. Really vast.
There are more stars, planets and moons out there
than even the most dedicated astronomer can count.
The study of space is a really exciting branch of
physics, known as **astrophysics**. Astrophysicists have
to invent ways to study things that are so far away
they'll probably never be able to travel to them.

Starry, starry night

A whole lot of nothing

Space, as its name suggests, is mostly just empty space. And empty really does mean empty – there isn't even any air in it, so you wouldn't be able to breathe. And away from any planets or stars, there isn't any gravity. Astronauts who take a space 'walk' actually just float.

Holes in space

When a huge star burns out and dies, it can collapse inwards, becoming a super-dense whirlpool known as a 'black hole'.

Black holes have such strong gravity that they suck everything in from a dying star – including the light. So they're only visible as 'gaps' in space.

No one knows what happens inside a black hole. Some scientists think they're portholes to parallel universes. But even if that were true, anyone entering one would be squashed into oblivion by the intense gravity before they could find out.

When you look up into the night sky, you're looking out into space. All the stars you can see are part of a group – or galaxy – named the Milky Way. If you could see it from far enough away, it would look like a swirling mass of milky-pale light. There are millions of other galaxies besides ours, and billions of other stars.

When you stargaze, you're also looking back in time. Every star (apart from the Sun) is so far away that even light – the speediest thing in the Universe – takes years to travel from them to us. In fact, astrophysicists actually measure distances across space in 'light years'. One light year is the distance light travels while a whole year passes on Earth – 9,460,730,472,600,000m.

The most distant stars in our galaxy are 100,000 light years away from Earth, and the Andromeda galaxy, which is quite near ours, is 2.5 million light years away. That means you're seeing it as it looked 2.5 million years ago.

Mind the gap!

This is a photograph of a galaxy called NGC 1300. It's similar in shape to our own galaxy, the Milky Way.

What's the Sun?

The Sun is just another star. It's not even a particularly big one — it only seems bigger and brighter than other stars because it's much closer to us. But it's still about a million times bigger than the Earth.

Like every other star, the Sun is an unbelievably hot ball of burning gases, which are squashed together, causing explosions which produce light and heat.

Why is night dark?

The Earth is constantly moving around the Sun, in a path known as an **orbit**. At the same time, the Earth constantly turns, like a spinning top, on its **axis** — an imaginary line through the middle of the planet.

A day is the time a planet takes to turn around once. On Earth, that takes 24 hours. So it's daytime on the side that's facing the Sun, and night on the other side where it's dark.

What causes the seasons?

The Earth's axis is at an angle to its orbit. When your part of the planet is tilted towards the Sun, it's summer. The Sun seems to shine more strongly, the days are longer, and nights are shorter. When you're tilted away from the Sun, it's winter. Nights are longer, days are shorter, and it's colder.

Don't look!

You should never look directly at the Sun — not even with sunglasses on, or through a camera or telescope. It could seriously damage your eyes.

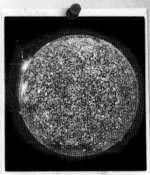

A photograph of the Sun taken through a telescope

See for yourself — the seasons

Shine a flashlight straight down at the ground. The ground will be lit up really brightly. This is how the Sun shines in summer.

Now shine the flashlight at an angle. The light will spread out more, and look paler. This is how the Sun shines in winter. When rays of sunlight are spread out, they're less warm.

In January, it's summer in the Earth's southern countries.

In June, it's summer in the Earth's northern countries.

Axis

North

South

What's the Moon?

The Moon is the second brightest object in the sky, after the Sun. But it's actually just a big lump of rock, and it doesn't give off any light at all. What we call moonlight is in fact sunlight, reflected off the Moon.

That's not to say the Moon isn't important. The Moon's gravity pulls on the Earth so much that it makes the sides of the planet bulge outwards a little bit. You can't really see the effect on solid land, but you can if you look at the sea: it pulls the oceans back and forth, causing the tides.

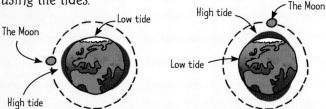

Men on the Moon

In 1961, the American President John F. Kennedy launched a space program named Apollo. He promised men would walk on the Moon before 1970.

The first Apollo spacecraft, Apollo 1, exploded on the launchpad in 1967, killing three men. But with only months until the end of the decade, in 1969, the program succeeded. Apollo 11 landed on the Moon.

The Apollo 11 crew – Neil Armstrong, Michael Collins and Buzz Aldrin

Neil Armstrong became the first man to walk on the Moon. He and fellow astronaut Buzz Aldrin spent two hours exploring the Moon's dusty surface.

Between 1969-1975, twelve Apollo astronauts visited the Moon. They're the only humans who've ever actually visited another place in space – so far...

Astronaut Alan Bean on the Moon in 1969

Why does the Moon change shape?

If you look up into the night sky, you'll see the Moon doesn't always look the same. Sometimes it's a round full Moon, and sometimes it's a barely-there crescent. The different shapes are called the **phases** of the Moon.

But the Moon isn't really changing shape at all. As the Moon orbits around the Earth, the Sun's rays hit it at different angles. People on Earth see more or less of the Moon depending on where it is in relation to the Sun.

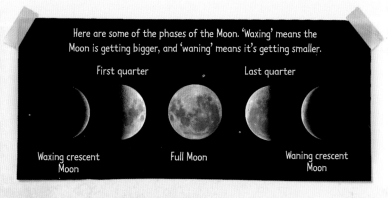

Here are some of the phases of the Moon. 'Waxing' means the Moon is getting bigger, and 'waning' means it's getting smaller.

First quarter   Last quarter

Waxing crescent Moon   Full Moon   Waning crescent Moon

Why is a year twelve months long?

The word 'month' comes from the word 'Moon'. One month is about the amount of time the Moon takes to go around the Earth.

The Moon orbits the Earth about twelve times a year, so there are twelve months in a year. But it doesn't make it around twelve times exactly. Every four years we have to adjust the length of a year so the Moon can catch up. An extra day is added to February, making a 'leap' year of 366 days.

Once in a blue moon...

In most years, there are 12 full moons, one for each calendar month. But every two or three years, there's a 13th full moon – often called a 'blue' moon – but it's actually the same colour as normal.

It was a dark and stormy day...

Sometimes, the Moon passes between the Earth and the Sun, and blocks out the Sun's light completely. This is called a **solar eclipse**. The Moon is a lot smaller than the Sun, but it's also a lot closer – so it seems to cover the Sun, and throw a shadow over part of the Earth.

During a total solar eclipse, it becomes cold and dark very quickly. Birds head to their nests, as they think night has come. In the past, people thought eclipses meant the end of the world was coming.

A life-saving eclipse

In 1503, explorer Christopher Columbus was shipwrecked on an island, and in need of food.

He knew that a lunar eclipse was about to occur, so he told the islanders that his God would get angry with them and make the Moon disappear if they didn't feed him.

Sure enough, as the Earth moved between the Sun and the Moon, the sky began to glow an angry red, and the Moon soon disappeared. Columbus got his food.

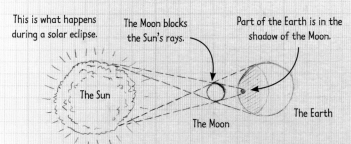

This is what happens during a solar eclipse.

The Moon blocks the Sun's rays.

Part of the Earth is in the shadow of the Moon.

The Sun

The Moon

The Earth

Lunar eclipses are less spectacular, but much more common. They happen when the Earth moves between the Sun and the Moon, blocking the Sun's light from the Moon – so the Moon seems to disappear.

Our Solar System

Planets are huge balls of matter that orbit a star. Some are made of solid rock; others are mostly made of gas. The Earth is just one of eight planets which orbit the Sun. Together, the Sun and the planets make up our **Solar System**. Our Sun isn't the only star with planets orbiting it – many other stars have them, too.

Each planet's orbit is a different size, which means it takes some of them longer to go around the Sun than others. One year is the amount of time it takes a planet to orbit the Sun once. So how long a year is depends on which planet you're on.

The centre of the Universe?

Until the 16th century, people thought the Earth was the centre of the Universe, and the Sun and the planets moved around it.

Then an astronomer named Copernicus suggested that the Earth moved around the Sun.

A scientist named Galileo agreed, and in 1632 he wrote a book about it.

Galileo's book got him in trouble with the Church, which taught that the Earth was at the centre of the Universe. Galileo was put under house arrest for the rest of his life.

Venus

The hottest planet, covered with gases so thick they would crush you to death – if they didn't poison you first.

Length of year: 225 Earth days
Length of day: 243 Earth days
Average temp.: 465°C
Moons: none

The Sun

The Sun is 99.8% of the mass of the Solar System – so everything else only makes up a measly 0.2% of it.

The asteroid belt

Thousands of bits of rock and metal which orbit the Sun between Mars and Jupiter. They can be as tiny as a pea, or as big as a city.

Mercury

Small rocky planet with no air to breathe.

Length of year: 88 Earth days
Length of day: 59 Earth days
Temperature: -170° to 427°C
Moons: none

Saturn

Completely made of gas, surrounded by rings made of lumps of rock and ice.

Length of year: 29 Earth years
Length of day: 10.5 Earth hours
Average temp: -178°C
Moons: 60 (that we know of)

Pluto

Until 2006, scientists classed far-off Pluto as a planet, but they now they call it a 'dwarf planet', because it's much smaller than the eight main planets.

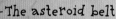

Many moons

A moon is a lump of rock that orbits a planet, just as planets orbit the Sun. The Earth only has one moon, but some planets have lots. Jupiter has at least 63, and there may be more astronomers haven't spotted yet.

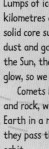

Big and far away

The planets on this page, and the distances between them, aren't shown to scale.

Jupiter

The biggest planet in the Solar System. The large red spot on its surface is a storm that's been raging for hundreds – maybe thousands – of years.

Length of year: 11.9 Earth years
Length of day: 9.9 Earth hours
Average temp: -153°C
Moons: at least 63

Neptune

Stormy planet with winds as fast as a jet plane.

Length of year: 164 Earth years
Length of day: 16 Earth hours
Average temp: -236°C
Moons: 13

Comets

Lumps of ice and rock, about 1-5 kilometres across. Comets have a solid core surrounded by a cloud of dust and gas. When they pass near the Sun, they reflect sunlight and glow, so we can see them.

Comets leave a trail of dust and rock, which rains down on Earth in a meteor shower when they pass through Earth's orbit.

Earth

Delightful planet, mostly covered in water, home to lots of interesting creatures, including humans.

Length of year: 365.25 days
Length of day: 24 hours
Temperature: from about -88°C to 58°C
Moons: one

Uranus

This planet has an axis that's much more tilted that the Earth's axis. It's practically on its side.

Length of year: 84 Earth years
Length of day: 17.24 Earth hours
Average temp: -213°C
Moons: 27 moons (that we know of)

Mars

If humans ever had to leave Earth, Mars would probably be the best place to move – even though it's horribly cold, and doesn't have any air. In fact, the American space agency NASA is currently planning a mission to visit Mars. If it goes ahead, the astronauts would be the first ever to have visited another planet.

Length of year: 685 Earth days
Length of day: about 40 minutes longer than a day on Earth
Average temp: -23°C
Moons: two little ones

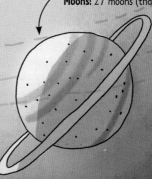

Part 6:
More about physics

Physics is such a huge subject that there are always plenty of new areas in it to explore. Turn the page to find out more about the discoveries physicists have made over the centuries, and how you can design and carry out your own physics experiments.

Physics through the ages

People have been studying how the *Universe* works for thousands of years. The word 'physics' comes from a Greek word, *physis*, meaning nature. All kinds of things were considered to be physics until the 16th century, including philosophy and chemistry. Here's the story of physics so far:

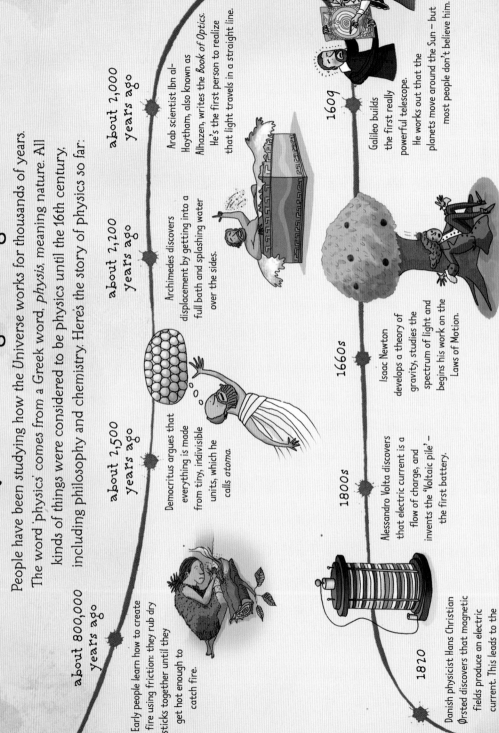

about 800,000 years ago

Early people learn how to create fire using friction: they rub dry sticks together until they get hot enough to catch fire.

about 2,500 years ago

Democritus argues that everything is made from tiny, indivisible units, which he calls *atoma*.

about 2,200 years ago

Archimedes discovers displacement by getting into a full bath and splashing water over the sides.

about 2,000 years ago

Arab scientist Ibn al-Haytham, also known as Alhazen, writes the *Book of Optics*. He's the first person to realize that light travels in a straight line.

1609

Galileo builds the first really powerful telescope. He works out that the planets move around the Sun – but most people don't believe him.

1660s

Isaac Newton develops a theory of gravity, studies the spectrum of light and begins his work on the Laws of Motion.

1800s

Alessandro Volta discovers that electric current is a flow of charge, and invents the 'Voltaic pile' – the first battery.

1820

Danish physicist Hans Christian Ørsted discovers that magnetic fields produce an electric current. This leads to the development of

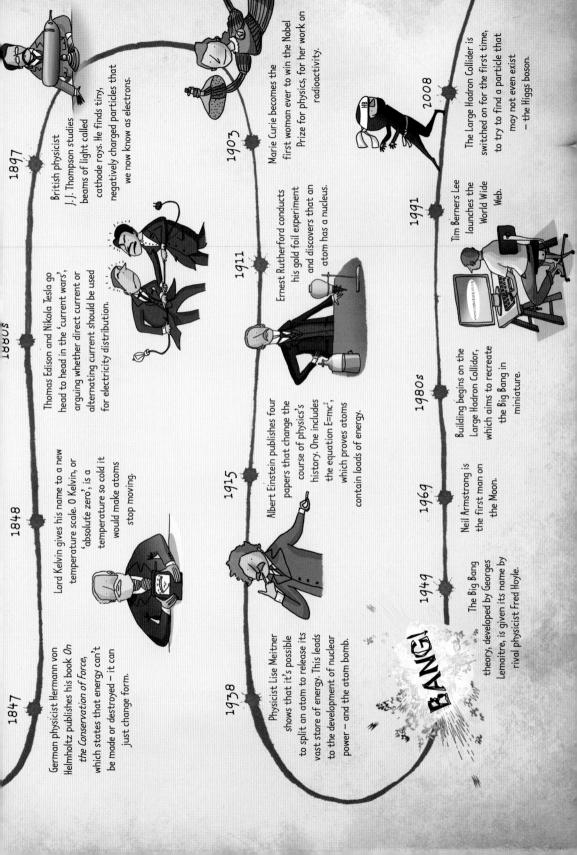

1847

German physicist Hermann von Helmholtz publishes his book *On the Conservation of Force*, which states that energy can't be made or destroyed – it can just change form.

1848

Lord Kelvin gives his name to a new temperature scale. 0 Kelvin, or 'absolute zero', is a temperature so cold it would make atoms stop moving.

1880s

Thomas Edison and Nikola Tesla go head to head in the 'current wars', arguing whether direct current or alternating current should be used for electricity distribution.

1897

British physicist J.J. Thompson studies beams of light called cathode rays. He finds tiny, negatively charged particles that we now know as electrons.

1903

Marie Curie becomes the first woman ever to win the Nobel Prize for physics, for her work on radioactivity.

1911

Ernest Rutherford conducts his gold foil experiment and discovers that an atom has a nucleus.

1915

Albert Einstein publishes four papers that change the course of physics's history. One includes the equation $E=mc^2$, which proves atoms contain loads of energy.

1938

Physicist Lise Meitner shows that it's possible to split an atom to release its vast store of energy. This leads to the development of nuclear power – and the atom bomb.

BANG!

1949

The Big Bang theory, developed by Georges Lemaitre, is given its name by rival physicist Fred Hoyle.

1969

Neil Armstrong is the first man on the Moon.

1980s

Building begins on the Large Hadron Collider, which aims to recreate the Big Bang in miniature.

1991

Tim Berners Lee launches the World Wide Web.

2008

The Large Hadron Collider is switched on for the first time, to try to find a particle that may not even exist – the Higgs boson.

What is science?

Science comes from the Latin word, *scientia*, meaning 'knowledge'. It is the study of how things work, and is divided into three areas:

Physics is the study of the laws that rule the Universe.

Chemistry is about the substances that make up the world.

Biology is the study of life.

How does physics work?

Physicists (and all other kinds of scientists too) come up with ideas that explain something about the world. They base those ideas on things they've seen, or that other physicists have written about.

Then they have to see if their ideas are right. To be a real scientist, it isn't enough to say that what you *think* is true, or that you believe it, or that it's common sense. You have to *prove* it's right (or at least, not wrong), by doing experiments that back it up. When an idea can be tested through experiments, it's called a **hypothesis**.

Professional scientists write about their experiments in journals, so other scientists around the world can try them too. If other experts agree there is enough evidence, the hypothesis becomes a **theory** — that means, it's the accepted, tested and most likely explanation of why something is the way it is.

How do experiments work?

An experiment must be a fair test of an idea.

1. Hypothesis
This is where you explain what your idea is. It also usually includes predictions of what you expect the results of the experiment to be.

2. Method
This describes how you're going to do the experiment. It includes a **control**, which is the 'normal' situation; and the experiment which is like the control but with one key difference. That way, if the results vary, you know it must be because of that one thing.

3. Results
These record the outcome of the experiment (including the control).

4. Conclusion
This is where you interpret the results. Did they support the hypothesis? Have you changed or rejected your hypothesis after seeing the results?

Here's an example of a simple scientific experiment:

1. Hypothesis
'The hotter water is, the easier it is to dissolve sugar in it.'

2. Method
Take three beakers, and label them A, B and C. Pour 1 litre of ice-cold water into beaker A, 1 litre of hot water into beaker B, and 1 litre of room temperature water into beaker C. Beaker C is the control. Add 25g of sugar to beaker A and stir the water. Count how many times you need to stir it until the sugar dissolves. Then do the same with beaker B and beaker C.

3. Results
The sugar in beaker B takes the least stirring to dissolve, and the sugar in beaker A takes the most.

4. Conclusion
The only difference between the beakers was the water temperature. So we can conclude that the hotter the water is, the easier it is to dissolve sugar in it. This supports the hypothesis.

However, there might be reasons why this experiment wouldn't work. For example, you might have stirred the water in the beakers at different speeds. It's really important to make sure that the water temperature is the only difference between the three beakers.

Are scientists ever wrong?

Yes, scientists get things wrong all the time! They may misinterpret the results of their experiments, or not be able to test ideas until the right technology is invented.

But what every good scientist wants most of all is to discover how things really work – even if that means admitting to mistakes along the way. So if their ideas are proved wrong, they're always prepared to change what they think, and move on.

> '**The one who seeks truth … submits to argument and demonstration**'
>
> This was the philosophy of one of the first people to use fair, rigorous experiments.
>
> Ibn al-Haytham, an 11th-century scholar, based his theories about light and vision on his own observations, rather than what people usually assumed was true.
>
> He argued that scholars shouldn't trust anyone's ideas without carefully considering the evidence for themselves.

Glossary

Words in *italics* have their own separate entries.

acceleration The rate at which an object's *velocity* changes.

alternating current (AC) *Current electricity* which constantly changes direction. The most widely used type of current.

amplitude The height of a *wave*.

astrophysicist A physicist who studies space.

atom The smallest building block of an *element*.

axis An imaginary line around which something (for example, a planet) spins.

Big Bang The theory that says the universe suddenly exploded into being.

centre of gravity The point through which the Earth's *gravity* acts on an object.

circuit A closed loop of wire around which *current electricity* can flow.

concave lens A *lens* with at least one surface bending inwards.

condensation When a gas changes into a liquid.

conduction When hotter *molecules* transfer heat to cooler *molecules* by bumping into them.

conductor A substance which allows heat or electricity to move through it.

convection When heat is transferred by moving *molecules*.

convex lens A *lens* with at least one surface bending outwards.

current electricity A flow of charged particles.

density How much *mass* an object has in relation to its *volume*.

direct current (DC) *Current electricity* which only flows in one direction. Supplied by batteries.

displacement The *volume* of water (or another substance) pushed out of the way by an object.

echo A sound *wave* which has been *reflected* off a surface and is heard after the original sound.

eclipse When light from the Sun or Moon is blocked off by an object moving in front of it.

electromagnet A magnet which only attracts metals when *current electricity* flows through it.

electromagnetic spectrum A family of *energy waves*, including heat and light, which all travel at the *speed of light*.

electron A tiny, negatively charged particle that *orbits* an *atom's* nucleus.

element The simplest type of substance, made up of only one type of *atom*.

energy The ability to do *work*.

evaporation When a liquid changes into a gas.

frequency The number of *waves* that pass a particular point every second. In sound, frequency determines how high- or low-pitched a noise is.

friction A *force* which opposes the motion of two objects rubbing against each other.

force A push or a pull which changes the motion or shape of an object.

fossil fuel A source of *energy* made from the fossilized remains of plants and animals.

galaxy A group of stars.

gravity A *force* which pulls all objects together. On Earth, it pulls everything downwards.

inertia When an object resists a change of *velocity*.

insulator A substance which resists heat or electricity moving through it.

kinetic energy Movement *energy*.

lens A *transparent* substance with at least one curved surface which *refracts* light, usually to help people see better.

machine An object which makes it easier to do *work*.

magnet An object that attracts some metals and attracts or repels other magnets.

magnetic field The area around a *magnet* in which objects are affected by *magnetic force*.

magnetic force The *force* which makes a *magnet* attract some metals and attract or repel other *magnets*.